Terence Davies

Contemporary Film Directors

Edited by Justus Nieland and Jennifer Fay

The Contemporary Film Directors series provides concise, well-written introductions to directors from around the world and from every level of the film industry. Its chief aims are to broaden our awareness of important artists, to give serious critical attention to their work, and to illustrate the variety and vitality of contemporary cinema. Contributors to the series include an array of internationally respected critics and academics. Each volume contains an incisive critical commentary, an informative interview with the director, and a detailed filmography.

A list of books in the series appears at the end of this book.

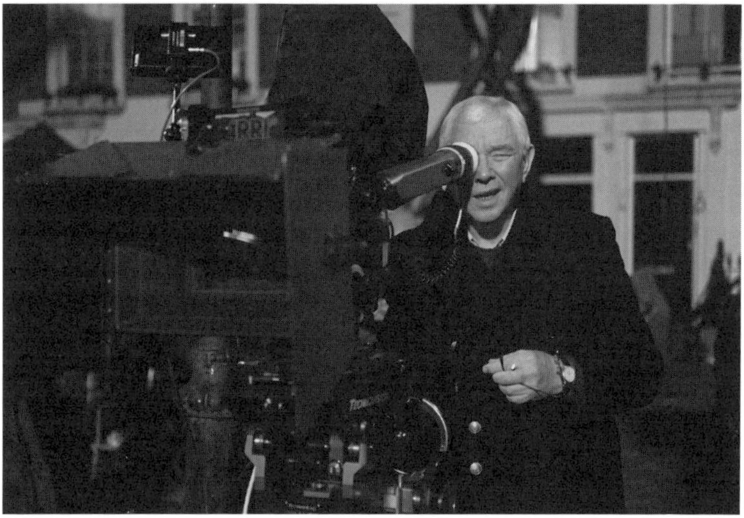

Terence Davies

Michael Koresky

**UNIVERSITY
OF
ILLINOIS
PRESS**
URBANA,
CHICAGO,
AND
SPRINGFIELD

© 2014 by the Board of Trustees
of the University of Illinois
All rights reserved
Manufactured in the United States of America
1 2 3 4 5 C P 5 4 3 2 1
∞ This book is printed on acid-free paper.

Frontispiece: Terence Davies on the set of *The Deep Blue Sea* (2011).

Library of Congress Cataloging-in-Publication Data
Koresky, Michael, 1979–
Terence Davies / Michael Koresky.
pages   cm. — (Contemporary film directors)
Includes bibliographical references and index.
Includes filmography.
ISBN 978-0-252-03861-7 (cloth : alk. paper) —
ISBN 978-0-252-08021-0 (pbk. : alk. paper) —
ISBN 978-0-252-09654-9 (e-book)
1. Davies, Terence, 1945– —Criticism and interpretation.
2. Davies, Terence, 1945– —Interviews. I. Title.
PN1998.3.D3815K68   2014
791.4302'33092—dc23   2014005895

Contents

Acknowledgments	ix
BATHED IN THE FADING LIGHT	1
The Fiction of Autobiography	18
The Elation of Melancholy	60
The Radical Traditional	89
The Fixity of Forward Motion	106
AN INTERVIEW WITH TERENCE DAVIES	125
Filmography	147
Bibliography	153
Index	159

Acknowledgments |

First of all, I'd like to thank Terence Davies for being so generous with his time and thoughts; I couldn't have realized this project without his support and eloquence. I'm unlikely to ever forget the chilly October afternoon I spent in his charmingly modest row house in Mistley, Essex, sipping tea while hearing him talk about his life and films. Thanks also to Davies's kind and enormously helpful assistant, John Taylor, always prompt and friendly in his responses to my surely nagging queries. I am enormously grateful to the editors, Justus Nieland and Jennifer Fay, whose elegantly considered and informed notes and suggestions consistently set me off on new and exciting paths, and to Daniel Nasset, who tirelessly shepherded this project to its final state. It is also safe to say that this volume would never have happened without the influence and motivation of my friend David T. Johnson; the guidance and encouragement of my coworkers at the Criterion Collection, especially Peter Becker, Elizabeth Helfgott, Kim Hendrickson, Brian McCreight, Casey Moore, Fumiko Tagaki, Anna Thorngate, and Jonathan Turell; or the hospitality of my colleague Julien Allen and his wife, Charlotte, both dear friends. I would also like to thank Duncan Petrie for his crucial feedback upon reading the manuscript, and Eric Hynes, Kent Jones, Adam Nayman, Nick Pinkerton, Jeff Reichert, Damon Smith, Andrew Tracy, and Genevieve Yue, all of whom are continual inspirations to me and who influenced this book in more ways than they might imagine. Finally, anyone who knows me knows that this book would have been impossible without Christopher Wisniewski, who supports, loves, inspires, and most importantly, challenges me every day.

Terence Davies

Bathed in the Fading Light

"I don't feel part of life. I always felt as though I were a spectator."
—Terence Davies

The cinema of the British director Terence Davies is one of contradictions—between beauty and ugliness, the real and the artificial, progression and tradition, motion and stasis. These opposites reflect a certain struggle, for the filmmaker and his characters, to make sense of a confusing and sometimes violent world. For Davies, this struggle constitutes a reckoning with his past, a highly personal account of a fractured childhood; for the viewer it has resulted in one of the richest, most idiosyncratic, and arrestingly experimental bodies of work put out by a narrative filmmaker. This struggle is particularly acute because Davies, a gay man who has long accepted his homosexuality yet has also often vocalized the shame he feels about it, is constantly negotiating issues of identity in his work—both his own and those of his characters. Davies's world is a personalized vision of the twentieth century refracted through a decidedly queer prism.

A recurring image in Davies's films shows someone staring out of a window. A character faces the camera, looking onto a world that has confounded, betrayed, or oppressed. This specific visual bestows great power on both his first film, 1976's forty-six-minute *Children*, and 2011's *The Deep Blue Sea*, his most recent feature at the time of this writing. The first is a spare, black-and-white work of tortured, fictionalized autobiography, recounting the filmmaker's traumatic coming-of-age in grim, mostly static compositions; the latter is an adaptation of a 1953 play by Terence Rattigan about a married woman's self-destructive affair, shot through with a seductive, rich classicism that could almost be called luxuriant. Worlds apart in many ways, the films are united by the manner in which their maker's presence is felt within them, never more strongly than in those images of the protagonist gazing out at us, past us, at a universe he or she doesn't understand, and which hasn't taken the time to understand the person contemplating it.

At the climax of *Children*, Davies's pubescent surrogate, Tucker (Philip Mawdsley), has been affected by twinned traumas: he is slowly becoming aware of his incipient homosexuality, and he has lost his father to pancreatic cancer. Though the director has shown us the older man writhing in pitiful agony, we have not been invited to feel sympathy for him: he has been depicted as a tyrant, beating Tucker's mother in a splenetic rage. Thus his death evokes in Tucker not sadness but mixed feelings of horror and joy, perhaps even more difficult emotions with which to reckon than had he merely been driven to mourn. With one shot—remarkable for its technical virtuosity and its ability to encapsulate warring feelings—Davies makes this moment unbearably vivid as well as metaphorically resonant. It is the morning of the funeral, and he has trained his camera on the front door of Tucker's Liverpool row house, the camera patient and still as the coffin is carried out. Tucker walks into the frame, flanked by his mother and a couple of unnamed female mourners. Their ghostly faces peer out from behind the window's cross-shaped grilles, which dominate the image. In a technical move that would prove uncommon in Davies's cinema, the camera slowly zooms out on this haunting tableau (Davies would later rely on tracking and crane shots rather than zooms for such flourishes); in this shot, Tucker's mouth breaks into a broad smile, one that only he could be aware of since the other mourners are positioned behind him. It's an eerie image, wholly incongruous with the melancholy scene, yet Davies's masterstroke is to come. The camera continues to zoom out, until the hearse enters the foreground; the coffin is mounted into the car from left to right, and as it slides into the back of the vehicle,

The erasure of a family in *Children*.

its motion literally erases Tucker and his mother from the shot as though marks wiped from a chalkboard. The shot is made possible via a double-reflection of the front door and a second window across the street; the image conveys an extraordinary sense of both negation (the family unit's erasure) and coming-into-being (Tucker's smile connoting the possibility of a newfound happiness). A line from the single most influential work of art in Davies's life, T. S. Eliot's *Four Quartets,* comes to mind: "In the end is my beginning."

The same sentiment could apply to the closing moments of *The Deep Blue Sea*. Though employing multiple flashbacks that give it the sense of a grand, time-hopping personal epic, the narrative proper takes place over the course of one day, following the night during which Hester (Rachel Weisz) attempts suicide via asphyxiation by gas heater. Over the film's unfolding twenty-four hours, Hester—who in the years immediately following the war has left her loving and reliable but dull husband, a prominent and wealthy judge, for a romance with a young and handsome but penniless and emotionally unstable former RAF pilot—has tried to reconcile, or at least comprehend, the opposed halves of her embattled life. Whether she has come to any greater understanding of herself by the end of the film is left ambiguous, but we do know this: she has, for this one morning at least, chosen life. She throws open the heavy curtains, flooding her dingy boarding-house apartment with sunlight. Davies cuts to an exterior shot of her standing in the window, and before the camera cranes down and away from her (in a reverse mirror image of the film's opening shot), we note the trace of a smile as Hester looks out. It is not as broad as Tucker's, but her expression is similar: conveying the need to move forward yet clearly haunted by the past.

Davies is a cinematic auteur in the classical sense, authoring films from an unmistakably personal aesthetic and thematic standpoint. And if any true auteur's protagonists are in some essential way their surrogates, then Tucker and Hester, wildly different beings at different points in their lives, are vivid incarnations of Davies himself. They exist at two disparate poles of his filmography, casting ambiguous smiles in the face of death. Joyous and melancholic, inside and outside, gazing at the world yet examining the self, moving forward but standing still, anticipating the future yet held by the past, they elucidate juxtapositions that reflect fundamental paradoxes—and as we'll see, the queering agents—around which the rest of this book will revolve. These are films that would seem to function within the most identifiable of British cinematic traditions—broadly, that of realism—yet are just as often defined by fantasy, surreality, and subjective truth; that excavate a painful personal past by locating warmth, wonder, and pockets of happiness within; that are informed by classical Hollywood and British narrative traditions but use them as starting points for more daring experimentations of the cinematic form; that dramatize the progression of time by evoking time's inherent falseness, implying that the present is simply an ever-persistent echo of the past and effectively illustrating Gilles Deleuze's notion that in the modern cinema images no longer are linked by rational cause and effect but rather more obscure, sensorial continuities.

Considering the influence they had on his cinema, Eliot's *Four Quartets*—the poet's final major work, widely regarded as a significant achievement in twentieth-century writing—provide a useful starting point for discussing Davies's particular kind of modernist memory film. Unifying four separate poems, three of which were composed in London during the darkest days of World War II, when the city was being bombarded by German air raids, *Four Quartets* (first published together as a book in 1943, two years before Davies was born) form a guttural, philosophical, and profoundly spiritual meditation on the nature of time and memory in what the author, who later in life had become an Orthodox Christian, perceived as an increasingly godless world. Each poem is named after a concrete place in Eliot's past that he has imbued with rich metaphorical meaning: the first, "Burnt Norton," invites the reader to contemplate the Edenic rose garden of a country estate and the enchanting and ominous memories it summons; "East Coker" is concerned in part with the artistic endeavor, specifically with how it helps us transcend the hopelessness of reality and escape the web of time; "The Dry Salvages," awash in water imagery, partly recalls Eliot's boyhood in Cape Ann, Massachusetts, to limn the edges of a baptismal eternity. Finally, with "Little Gidding," Eliot tries to find peace in the attempt to reconcile the contradictory impulses inherent in the flow of life. As the Eliot scholar Russell Kirk writes, "*Four Quartets* point out the way to the Rose Garden that endures beyond time, where seeming opposites are reconciled" (241). Opposites also provide the philosophical foundation for Davies's cinema, yet unlike Eliot, Davies outright rejects religious dogma, and therefore he is not able to reconcile the warring aspects of his life via a transcendent, sustaining spirituality. Nevertheless, the ultimate optimism in Eliot's *Four Quartets*—which vibrate with hope, the possibility for human salvation and immortality through religion, without ever preaching a specific theology—appeals to Davies, as do the poems' critique of the modern consciousness and their evocative, highly musical rhythm and structure. The past, present, and future all exist on one plane throughout the *Four Quartets*, as is the case with many of Davies's films, which revolve and undulate rather than move in a straight line.

Davies's films evoke Eliot's words, "Time the destroyer is time the preserver." It is essential to recognize and embrace the central paradoxes of Davies's body of work to fully grasp and interpret it—and to realize how he has radicalized an essentially mainstream narrative cinema. Visually and sonically unorthodox, Davies's films are highly aestheticized, and the curious nature of their approaches makes them difficult to situate. (If there has been occasional criticism of their distancing visual strategies, it has centered on the oddness of their hovering between realism and stylization—for instance, John Caughie was harsh on *The Long Day Closes* for what he viewed as "an aestheticization of drabness," which he found at times to be "emotionally exploitative" [13].) Yet his defiance of easy genre categorization, his refusal to slot his films into established British or American cinematic traditions, and the manner in which he has put his distinct stamp on other writers' material all eloquently speak to the way Davies has subtly created a queered filmography. He comes by his gentle radicalism naturally and genuinely; rather than setting out to complicate the unwritten rules of modern moviemaking, he seems to construct films as a way of locating a hidden lyricism—to create a poetics of trauma that narrows viewers' common perceptions of the gulf between pain and pleasure, joy and grief, memory and fantasy. In so doing, he forces an unsettling destabilizing effect on his own cinema; the clearest way to explain his films' essential queerness is to say that he seems to place them in recognizable generic forms, only to delegitimize those very forms. The word "queer"—a once-demeaning term used against gays and lesbians to negatively identify difference that was recouped in the early 1990s as a politically charged emblem of positive self-identification by those who were marginalized by it—describes a defiance to heteronormatively established categories of sexual identity, dissolving boundaries between male and female, gay and straight. We might say that Davies's cinema, by virtue of its resistance to set aesthetic and political cinematic rules, similarly refuses either/or binaries. It is perhaps crucial to note that I am employing the term "queer," which has been utilized in many ways across multiple disciplines, in a two-pronged sense, both in terms of the director's homosexuality, reflected in the identity politics of many of his films, and to illustrate how his work deviates from the formal and cultural concerns of his cinematic contemporaries.

This queerness—the neither/nor quality—might help account for why Davies, despite the acclaim with which nearly all of his works have been met and the place of honor to which he has ascended in the annals of contemporary British cinema (he's "regarded by many as Britain's greatest living film director," wrote the *London Evening Standard*'s Nick Roddick in 2008), remains understudied at serious length; meanwhile, he has historically had difficulty getting official funding for his projects from governmental arts councils, further contributing to his status as an industry outsider. Various chapters in both popular and more academically oriented film-studies anthologies have been devoted to him over the past two decades, but Wendy Everett's invaluable *Terence Davies* (2001) for the Manchester University Press series British Film Makers remains the only previous existing English-language book-length study of the director's work. The reason for what is surely a critical oversight cannot simply be Davies's relatively small output: the seven features he has made at the time of this writing puts him in the same general category as such world-cinematic titans as Terrence Malick (six films), Andrei Tarkovsky (seven), Wong Kar-wai (ten), and Stanley Kubrick (thirteen), all known for the extended length of time they take between projects, and all subjects of numerous published critical studies—and all of them, like Davies, evincing a clear aesthetic unity across their oeuvres. And neither can Davies's essential invisibility in the U.S. academic press be due to a matter of stateside inaccessibility, as his works were all at one time or another afforded distribution from major independent companies, theatrically and on home video.

Rather, I would argue that the reason for the lack of widespread scholarly analysis of Davies's works is due to the difficulty of their unfashionably personal, contradictory queer natures, as well as the odd detachment with which they uncover deeply emotional states of being. A 1990 article by the U.S. critic Jonathan Rosenbaum in the British magazine *Sight & Sound* testifies to the inability of Davies's 1988 feature *Distant Voices, Still Lives* to connect with American audiences: "It was probably the relative absence of plot—the ne plus ultra of commercial filmmaking—that deprived the movie of the larger audience it could and should have had, even if this absence permits a wholeness and an intensity to every moment that is virtually inaccessible to narrative filmmaking" ("Are You Having Fun?" 99). The dramatic outlines of Davies's most personal films are universally relatable, but the abstractness with which he lays bare and interprets his traumas on the screen makes them opaque, even alien. Despite his most typical works being seemingly based in a recognizable idiom (broadly, the personal-memory film), they are not entirely legible as such. Upon deeper analysis, his films become puzzling works that skirt the lines between autobiography and fantasy, reality and fiction, radicalism and conservatism—each of those, incidentally, categories in which critics and academics prefer to place films.

Though his films have been explored at eloquent and revealing length in Everett's book, I aim to focus more on the distinct emotional quandaries these films evoke in the viewer and to propose that their tonal and political in-betweenness is a form of cinematic queering. Through my exploration of their contradictions in the sections that follow, I will suggest that these films function within seemingly recognizable generic parameters only to then explode and thus queer conventional notions of narrative cinema. Whereas Everett's book took the form of a chronological study of the director's work, I am more interested in teasing out the connections and cross-references between his films in a less linear, more holistic fashion. Furthermore, Everett's volume, published in 2001, necessarily could not have dealt with Davies's two most recent films, *Of Time and the City* and *The Deep Blue Sea,* rich and significant texts that further elucidate the tenor and subtext of the director's entire oeuvre, while also moving him into new realms (broadly, documentary and melodrama). Also, in focusing on what I see as the central paradoxes of Davies's films, I will attempt to imply a more specifically queer reading than Everett had, to impart a sense that all of his seemingly opposed aesthetic and ideological cinematic traits work in surprising tandem to create a radical portrait of a fractured gay identity.

I aim not simply to delve into the textually or even subtextually gay aspects or details of the films but rather to propose that, in their entirety, and in the odd juxtapositions that fasten them together, they are imbued with—and perhaps *defined* by—a queer sensibility. Davies's homosexuality—a source of anguish for him—is not merely incidental to any of these films, even those that elide any explicit reference to same-sex desire. These matters are also not so easy to parse. There are a variety of dimensions to Davies's highly modernist queer aesthetic, and they are at turns related to desire, identity, politics, and time. For instance, alongside his impulse toward autobiography seems to sit a drive for self-negation; he's inviting us to share his dreams and fears and privileging us to witness approximations of his past experiences, yet at the same time disallowing simple emotional readings of those experiences by foregrounding his own perspective as that of an outsider, a stranger in a strange land of his own making. Such aesthetics connect to one of the most essential aspects of Davies's queerness: his status as a social outcast, a position related, variously, to his sexuality, his placement within (but mostly outside of) the mainstream film industry, and his devotion to outmoded pop-cultural signifiers, the traces of which appear in all of his films, often giving them the sense of emanating from an earlier—and, crucially, politically unfashionable—time and place.

With their constant tonal negotiations, Davies's films exist in a curious space between fondness for the past and fear of it, a positioning that makes us aware of the social exclusion that the director felt as both an adolescent and as a formerly sexually active adult (Davies claims to be celibate today), which is a defining feeling of queerness. As a result, Davies, a filmmaker particularly preoccupied with the representation of time in cinema, carves out a peculiar, queer temporality, locating his films in a space that exists *outside* of the flow of culturally sanctioned, positively identified, procreatively fueled "normal time." Time itself is reconstituted in Davies's cinema, whether fragmented or slowed down, either outpacing or trailing behind social norms; the inexorable pull of forward motion butts heads with a nagging, unavoidable emotional and physical stasis.

Aesthetically, Davies's queerness can be located in a series of distancing strategies that effectively put us viewers, and Davies, at a remove from the narratives, so that we are like Davies when he says, "I always felt as though I were a spectator" (qtd. in Everett 217). This is achieved through, variously and not exclusively, discordant sound-image combinations, hyperstylized visual compositions, and appropriations of mainstream, often Hollywood but also classic British, images and music, repurposed so that they both blend into Davies's narratives and work at meaningful cross purposes with them. It is fair to say that many of his films, obsessed with outmoded pop-culture paraphernalia Davies associates with his childhood, are subtly imbued with a camp sensibility, even as they are in dead earnest about their subject matter. There is an occasional exaggeration of effect, or at least luxuriousness, in the ways they both revel in and interrogate mainstream studio-film forms that can occasionally evoke the work of Kenneth Anger and Andy Warhol, especially when the explicitly gay bedrock of desire his films are founded on rises to the surface.

It needs to be emphasized that a main reason for Davies not yet being confirmed as an important queer auteur is that his films and his persona are hopelessly out of step with a scholarship and politics of queerness that is largely driven by notions of empowerment and pride. Critical queer-theory discourse arose in academia, within and outside of cinema-studies circles, at a moment in the early 1990s that coincided with the increasing mainstreaming of homoeroticism and the discussion of homosexual civil rights, both partly responses to the AIDS crisis. Yet as a discipline, it has more to do with social construction than gay liberation, and we must separate it from political rhetoric if we are to fruitfully situate Davies—a man who has told an interviewer in 2011, "Being gay has ruined my life" (Clarke)—as an important queer auteur. Davies's films, importantly, stand against the norm in terms of production, aesthetics, and thematics, even if that stance is not *defiant,* a term we might more often hear used in discussions of work by more identifiably "queer" filmmakers from the United Kingdom and the United States, such as Derek Jarman, Isaac Julien, and Todd Haynes, or even in such cornerstone gay British films as Stephen Frears's *My Beautiful Laundrette* (1985) and *Prick Up Your Ears* (1987) and Neil Jordan's *The Crying Game* (1992). These celebrated works, though not directed by gay artists, more outwardly engage with the politics of gender and sexuality and thus seem of a piece with modes of thought in academic and mainstream circles. In comparison, Davies's work is not easily situated in any contemporary, politicized queer discourse and may seem quaint, or worse, retrograde; his films do not argue on behalf of the legitimacy or naturalness of homosexuality. (It is worth noting that Davies doesn't rate a single mention in the New Queer Cinema trailblazer B. Ruby Rich's 2013 compendium *New Queer Cinema: The Director's Cut*.)

In other words, to definitively assert Davies's queerness is to place a not consciously progressive artist in a necessarily progressive field of study. Yet as Heather Love might argue, if her book *Feeling Backward: Loss and the Politics of Queer History* is evidence, Davies's acknowledgment of his own social stigma, and his inability to move past it, should hardly disqualify him as a queer artist. She writes, "Texts or figures that refuse to be redeemed disrupt not only the progress narrative of queer history but also our sense of queer identity in the present" (8); Love later explains that to deny such figures their place in the field of study is tantamount to "a disavowal of crucial aspects of this history and of the conditions of queer existence in the present" (17). Davies is such a figure, a man who came of artistic age in a socially liberal and more permissive era but whose work stands as a strangely conflicted testament to an earlier time in his life marked by great social conservatism and resultant despair.

Yet rarely has a gay feature filmmaker so completely and insistently plumbed the depths of his own embattled psyche while placing it in a concrete sociopolitical framework. Davies is surely a representative of what Love calls "modernity's backward children," a nonpejorative classification of queerness. His voice is unfashionable, perhaps, but also essential. There are simply no other personal-memory films quite like these, which reveal a cumulative and highly modern meditation on the construction of the self and its placement within larger social and cultural fabrics—the former being the contexts of family, school, and work, and the latter defined through the films' many cultural references, from movies to classical and popular music to poetry. For most of Davies's career as a director, and certainly its crucial, profoundly personal first half, from 1976 to 1992, these were located within the memories of his hometown of Liverpool, though as his filmography evolved and expanded, they rippled out to encompass not only London but also the foreign worlds of America's southern Bible Belt and New York City. Davies is mostly known for those works that fictionalized his own upbringing, and he has insisted that his films only reflect his own subjective truth, but they are hardly hermetic: in their sensitivity and primal emotionality, they paint on a wider canvas. A humanistic and poignant thread runs from *Children* through *The Deep Blue Sea*, common themes and contradictions that I will sketch in these introductory pages and explore at greater length in the sections that follow. Each film speaks to a world struggling to emerge from the psychic trauma of war or personal abuse.

Davies's cinema has defied easy categorization from the very start. In fact, his first official feature can hardly be termed a feature at all. *The Terence Davies Trilogy*, as it was called when released in 1984, is a compilation of three black-and-white shorts shot on 16mm over the course of seven years—*Children* (1976), *Madonna and Child* (1980), and *Death and Transfiguration* (1983)—all of which evince compositional poise and thematic audacity. The most strongly gay-oriented films of Davies's career, these were made years before there was anything approaching an alternative queer-cinema movement. The *Trilogy*'s importance to Davies's artistic mission is solidified by his choice to further explore its main character, milieu, theme, and triparite structure in his only novel, *Hallelujah Now* (1983), which similarly delves into its protagonist's profound guilt and trauma over his homosexuality in an achronological, stream-of-conscious manner that effectively destabilizes the present.

With his next two films, Davies continued to excavate his past, breaking up time in even more radical ways. *Distant Voices, Still Lives* (1988) and *The Long Day Closes* (1992), companion pieces of a sort, and the works on which the director's reputation largely lies, are woven tapestries of sounds and images, dreams and desires of a specifically working-class milieu that both evoke and fly in the face of the British school of realism that defined Davies's national cinema, from John Grierson and Humphrey Jennings's groundbreaking experiments in documentary in the 1930s and 1940s to the "kitchen-sink dramas" of the 1950s and 1960s to the "heritage" and new-realist films of the 1980s and 1990s, typified by Merchant-Ivory and Mike Leigh, respectively. While Davies adheres to a certain verisimilitude in his direction of actors in these films, his stylized cinematography and radical, dreamlike editing helps them dispense with the realism audiences would come to expect. In their clear move away from these traditions, *Distant Voices, Still Lives* and *The Long Day Closes* captured the attention and admiration of the

British film community; their unorthodox aesthetic techniques were acknowledged as evidence of a singular artistic voice, but at the same time, their autobiographical nature led many critics to pigeonhole Davies as a filmmaker interested strictly in his own past, a charge that would prove increasingly false as his career unfolded.

Distant Voices, Still Lives is aesthetically distinguished by two radical choices that set it dramatically apart from other family-memory films of the era (John Boorman's *Hope and Glory* [1987] is an excellent concurrent example in the United Kingdom; while Ettore Scola's *The Family* [1987] and Barry Levinson's *Avalon* [1990] make for more sentimental evocations of similar themes of generational loss from other countries, Italy and the United States, respectively.) The first is its expressive camera technique, which is made up of many static tableau-like compositions, punctuated by elegant tracking shots, the combination of which creates a dreamlike space that hangs somewhere between the authentic and the artificial. This almost constant negotiation of verisimilitude and constructedness heightens the viewer's sense that he or she is taking part in the filmmaker's subjective truth, a version of a reality affected by the magnifications and alterations of memory, whether idealized or deprecated.

The second way Davies's film represents a radical move away from traditional forms of fictional narrative is in its use of music. The whole of *Distant Voices, Still Lives* is constructed of seemingly disconnected scenes, threaded together by a complex series of voiceovers, popular songs and religious hymns, and, occasionally, synched dialogue that is used to sound-bridge disparate spaces. The most memorable sounds that bring together the film's many shards as well as create a more thematic harmony, however, are the popular radio tunes or ditties sung on-camera by its many characters. Entire sequences are made up strictly of these songs, whether performed as solos or singalongs, in the family's parlor or in the neighborhood pub. Similarly revealing the specters of the director's haunted childhood via a collage-like conglomeration of memories and pop-cultural references, *The Long Day Closes* brought Davies himself back into the equation. Front and center is Bud, a dour-faced boy on the verge of a puberty all the more traumatic for the explosion of homosexual desire that comes with it; unlike *Distant Voices, Still Lives*, in which the past is a malleable compound made up of the perspectives of multiple characters, this film emanates from a single consciousness.

The evolution of Davies's career up to this point would make one wonder whether fragmented memories were all he was capable of summoning. His next film, though a wild departure in many ways, did not provide easy answers. *The Neon Bible* (1995), adapted from John Kennedy Toole's slim bildungsroman about a sensitive boy's coming-of-age in the deep American South, represented a striking change of milieu for Davies, yet many of the director's already established hallmarks were in full view: taciturn young male protagonist, colorful and more outspoken older relative, the tyrannies of bullies and teachers, the comfort of movies, the birth of religious skepticism. If this alien landscape introduced a new (and probably healthy) awkwardness in Davies's filmmaking, it also resulted in a singular hybrid of Davies's poetic British lyricism and stoic American gothic. Davies's long, steady tracking shots and unbroken single takes register as dissociated and surreal when reconfigured into a Georgia-shot tale that features one character's dramatic descent into madness and another's violent, climactic killing.

The Neon Bible met with a cool response from critics and audiences; his next project brought him further from the well-trod territory of the memory film, and fully into the warm embrace of the cinematic community. *The House of Mirth* (2000), his pristine and chilling adaptation of Edith Wharton's first novel, set in a viperous, upper-class, turn-of-the-century New York City, features his most atypical subject matter thus far. *The House of Mirth* is an undeniable, elegant triumph in terms of storytelling, performance, and imagery. Yet the film's sheen of decorum masks what is essentially a horror movie, albeit one in which words are swiftly and efficiently used as deadly weapons, and in which the moral righteousness of its tragic heroine accelerates her downfall. By the time he made *The House of Mirth*, Davies was so known for these experiments in memory that, as he said, "I wanted to prove that I could write a linear narrative in which you seed things that pay off" (Fuller, "Summer's End" 55). Not only is the film's narrative told in a linear fashion, it moves forward with a scary inexorability, one scene following another with brutally gradual momentum. As in Davies's childhood films, there seems to be an almost constant fear (of being rejected, of being *found out*) simmering beneath *The House of Mirth.*

Whereas *The House of Mirth* is a remarkably faithful adaptation of Wharton's book, in which most noticeable alterations (the amalgamation of two supporting characters for dramatic economy, the excising of a small climactic scene) were ultimately slight, *The Deep Blue Sea* is a dramatic rethinking of Terence Rattigan's play, maintaining its basic structural through-line but using it as a foundation for experimentations in cinematic time and memory. That *The Deep Blue Sea* diverges so much from the original Rattigan text is particularly surprising in light of the fact that the project was developed with funding from the Sir Terence Rattigan Charitable Trust on the occasion of the playwright's centenary. Yet with carte blanche from producers to take liberties in his adaptation ("The Rattigan Trust told me after I'd done a tentative first draft, 'Be radical!' So I was," he told Geoff Andrew in *Sight & Sound* [24]), Davies made a film that could be called a reimagining of the source text. *The Deep Blue Sea* is thus wholly unorthodox as a tribute, yet in its fidelity to both Rattigan's spirit and to Davies's integrity (the director found much in the original play either implausible or uncinematic), it is perhaps the most expressive and cohesive film based on a Rattigan play. Furthermore, Davies's artistic sensibilities accentuate the implicit queerness in the original work; when paired with *The House of Mirth*'s Lily, *The Deep Blue Sea*'s Hester seems all the more fascinating as a source of queer identification.

Before he made *The Deep Blue Sea*, Davies embarked on a film that is singular in his oeuvre while at the same time furthers many ideas present in his other works. *Of Time and the City* (2008), Davies's single nonfiction film as well as his only one partially shot and edited on digital video, was made as part of a microbudget initiative called Digital Departures. Commissioned as a work of historical documentary for the city of Liverpool (the initiative was partly backed by the Liverpool Culture Company), Davies's film, unsurprisingly, turned out to be something far more personal—and critical—than a simple tribute; instead he created a patchwork of intimate revelations and reminiscences that are crosshatched with a wider historical and sociopolitical interrogation of Liverpool, from the 1950s of his childhood to the city as it stands in the first decade of the twenty-first century. Davies's take on Liverpool is subjective—it's an untenable place of the mind that exists even more vividly in his recollections than in the preexisting stock footage that makes up most of the film's visuals. *Of Time and the City* is bracing in its rejection of several common documentary practices, eschewing impersonal third-person narration in favor of Davies's own poignant tones (alternately honeyed and barbed-tongued) and refusing to contextualize or identify much of what we see via onscreen text or more direct voiceover. Thus even Davies's seemingly simple pocket-sized tribute to the hometown of his lost childhood becomes a highly complex, unorthodox work of nonfiction, in which one man's experience of his city's changing landscape is inextricable from the shame he felt over his own sexual coming-of-age or the joy he receives from recalling certain songs or movies—in other words, Davies's sense memory here becomes *the* memory of Liverpool.

Davies's relatively small output for such a long career is not by choice (for contrast, look at another filmmaker who's worked in the same basic stretch of years as Davies, the more commercial filmmaker Neil Jordan, who managed to direct seventeen features between 1982 and 2012). Funding for Davies's films has been difficult to raise, and the director has been notoriously outspoken on the subject, never shying away from denouncing the state of the contemporary British film industry following the government's destruction of the British Film Institute Production Board ("Now if a young filmmaker wants to use cinema as a form of expression and an art form, where do they go? How do they get it off the ground?" he asked in a 2006 interview with *The Guardian* [Hattenstone, "Bigmouth," 5]) and bemoaning his outsider status within it. The eight years between *The House of Mirth* and *Of Time and the City* constituted Davies's most prolonged, sharply felt absence from the film scene, even though *Mirth*'s major critical and commercial success seemed to indicate that new doors would open for him. Instead, one project after another fell through, including a romantic comedy titled *Mad about the Boy* and adaptations of the books *Sunset Song* by Lewis Grassic Gibbon (which Davies hoped would be heading into preproduction at the time of this writing) and *He Who Hesitates* by Ed McBain. Unlike *The Trilogy, Distant Voices, Still Lives, The Long Day Closes, The Neon Bible,* and *The House of Mirth,* all of which were projects he shepherded from the outset, *The Deep Blue Sea* and *Of Time and the City* were suggested to him by others. This ultimately doesn't make them any less personal, but it does give us a sense of the difficulties Davies has had in getting his own projects made and how important it has been in the current state of the industry, so focused on the box-office bottom line, for him to take advantage of such opportunities.

That Davies continues to have these sorts of struggles is perhaps in keeping with an artist who prevails despite, or indeed because of, emotional setbacks. "Without all that suffering, there wouldn't have been any films," he said in a 1992 interview (Dixon 193). The beauty that emerges from such pain reveals a method of reappropriating the past that we might call "queer" in the way it reconstitutes shards of Davies's cultural and familial detritus into new forms. That his art is empowering in its expression of sexual and social difference and at the same time stuck in a mode one could associate with vicitimization helps define the central contradictions that fuel Davies's cinema. This book endeavors to separate Davies's aesthetics into four discrete paradoxes, which I have titled the Fiction of Autobiography, the Elation of Melancholy, the Radical Traditional, and the Fixity of Forward Motion. By examining each of these, which range from matters thematic to temporal, literal to metaphysical, poetic to political, I hope to make vivid the affective queerness that fuels this director's extraordinary career. Heather Love might argue that queerness itself is marked by such juxtapositions: "Queers face a strange choice: is it better to move on toward a brighter future or to hang back and cling to the past? Such divided allegiances result in contradictory feelings: pride and shame, anticipation and regret, hope and despair" (27).

I have already laid out the specifics of Davies's career in a largely chronological fashion; this seems necessary at the outset, as knowledge of his progression from a filmmaker strictly interested in coming to terms with and reimagining his and his family's past to one fascinated by the challenges of adapting other artists' work paves the way for a better understanding of his unofficial artistic mission. However, in tribute to a subject whose most distinct, overtly personal films reject straightforward cause-and-effect trajectories, I will proceed by examining Davies's career in a nonlinear fashion, using commonalities and threads to jump back and forth throughout his filmography. His films are whirlpools of memories, summoned lovingly or with regret, images of agony and pleasure, life and death, melody and silence, and the linkages between them promise to provide even more insight—into Davies's interior world, yes, but also into cinema's potential to evoke contradictory emotional states simultaneously—than separate analyses of each ever could.

Despite their constant spiraling, there's a nagging, impenetrable stillness that grounds Davies's work, which one does not feel in the films of other directors so attracted to themes of time and memory, such as Alain Resnais, Terrence Malick, or Wong Kar-wai, whose films are boldly restless. Davies's characters are creatures who exist, as Eliot wrote in *The Four Quartets,* "at the still point of the turning world." They remain fixed at the center of all this roiling memory, existing in a present that is not a present but a compendium of sensations and images from the past. This erasure of a concrete Now brings Davies in close kinship with T. S. Eliot, his artistic idol and poetic ideal. Yet it also has wrought something distinctly, purely cinematic—a visual evocation of a world at once awash in pleasure, gripped by fear, and always aglow with the possibilities of a past that might never have existed at all.

The Fiction of Autobiography

Not far into Terence Davies's *Of Time and the City,* the narrator-director cheerfully intones: "If Liverpool didn't exist it would have to be invented." In the film, Davies identifies the source of the quote as the French artist Felicien de Myrbach. The sentiment is inscribed in Liverpool's St. George's Hall, a local landmark we soon see onscreen, and which the director describes in the interview that concludes this book as "the largest Greco-Roman neoclassical building in Europe." The quote eloquently expresses not only Davies's strategies in constructing this nonfiction portrait of the city of his youth but also his cinematic approach throughout his entire career. Says the director, "I suppose what [the quote] means is that even when you move away from it, it's still very much part of your imagination. When most Liverpudlians move away, and a lot of them do, they recreate that city as they remember it, and as they didn't remember it" (Hillis). *Of Time and the City* is a re-creation of Davies's hometown as he remembers—and doesn't remember—it; the abundance of found archival footage taken on Liverpool's streets that makes up the film does provide a historical portrait of a place, but more importantly it serves as backdrop for Davies's specific experience of it. This is reminiscent of most of Davies's films, which present information in seemingly autobiographical terms—as reflections of a certain reality—only to purposely distort or reimagine that reality as a way of getting at a greater, poetic truth. By overturning expectations of what nonfiction filmmaking is taken to be in the early part of the twenty-first century, Davies, with *Of Time and the*

City, reveals the ambiguous nature of his overall cinematic project—a recontextualization of the familiar, and a personalizing of the historical. As Jim Ellis writes, "Cinema is a particular way of viewing the world; for Davies, it offers the best representation of one version of a queer consciousness" ("Temporality" 174). History inevitably cooperates in the shaping of that queer consciousness.

In "The Fiction of Autobiography," I will map out the specifics of Davies's filmography and biography, and also go on to establish the manner in which he complicates these particulars, in order to better illustrate in later sections how Davies turns his themes and preoccupations into aesthetics and philosophy. It is important to note that even though shame and stigma have necessarily played a role in shaping his cinematic persona, Davies is not easily reducible to the image of the traumatized artist—a filmic Francis Bacon, if you will. As I hope to make clear, the contradictions inherent in his approach to movies flow out of trauma but give voice to an array of richly crisscrossing feelings, crescendos made up of both darkness and light. Davies is undeniably a survivor—of abuse, of crippling religious and sexual guilt—yet his work has never neglected to magnify the losses of queer history, even if implicitly.

"Come closer now and see your dreams," says Davies by way of a prologue for *Of Time and the City*, beckoning us as a deep-red curtain rises silently in a dark space that feels like a theater of the mind. Then, so as not to mistake his intent: "Come closer now and see *mine*." No detached ethnography, *Of Time and the City* is a ruminative and wistful journey into a past that for Davies is always present. Even though it shows a humane focus on the working-class people who have populated Liverpool for decades, the film is largely about Davies, which means that the director's recollections of his own stirring pubescent desires and confessions of distaste for rock-and-roll music and the pomp of the British royal family sit squarely alongside poetic musings on the cultural degradation of a city amidst increasing modernization and an exquisite socioeconomic portrait of the ever-struggling working classes. It becomes difficult to separate the personal from the political in the film, as Davies's narration places both on the same continuum.

In visual terms, *Of Time and the City* is most fascinated by architecture—how we interact with it, and how it defines landscape, character, and national and local identity. Liverpool's buildings, from its terraced working-class row houses to its municipal establishments, are the clearest evidence of the simultaneous development and decay that are the twinned hallmarks of any Western city throughout the twentieth century, especially those bombarded by the events of World War II. Davies most memorably expresses this ironic reverse development in a three-and-a-half-minute sequence that charts the demolition of the city's slums in the 1960s and 1970s to make way for low-income high-rises. Wholly without narration, and accompanied by Jerome Kern's "The Folks Who Live on the Hill," as sung in an ethereal 1957 recording by Peggy Lee, the sequence at once comments on what Davies sees as increasingly common urban blight, pays tribute to the working class from which he hails, and intimates the erasure of his own past. In fact, it was the conception of this sequence that convinced Davies that he could pursue the project, his first documentary, at all. Says the producer Solon Papadopoulos of this sequence, "Once he'd got that image in his head, he thought there was a film to be made: that was the moment, the catalyst" (qtd. in Corless, "Formula Free" 47). While he doesn't make the inspiration explicit, this bravura section of the film could be a concrete visualization of the opening metaphor of "East Coker," the second of Eliot's *Four Quartets*: "In succession / Houses rise and fall, crumble, are extended / Are removed, destroyed, restored, or in their place / Is an open field, a factory, or a by-pass."

The Liverpool of Davies's past is gone. "Now I'm an alien in my own land," he mourns near the end of the film. Liverpool is not only a specific past but also *the* past for Davies, therefore impossible to recoup as anything but a memory, an ideal, and a fantasy. This distinguishes *Of Time and the City* as more a work of imagination than a strict documentary. In the absence of a tenable extant connection to the place of his youth, Davies must create a narrative around it—it has to be invented. Though the film was funded to be a celebration of Liverpool on the occasion of the city's status as the European Capital of Culture for 2008, Davies ended up making both a personal film and an occasionally sharp-tongued social critique that didn't honor a city's legacy so much as excavate its ghosts, focusing mostly on its working poor. Furthermore, Davies does not seem interested in providing contextualizing historical information on Liverpool, so the universe as depicted in the film often comes across as mindscape more than landscape. He said at the time of its

Liverpool's houses rise and fall
in *Of Time and the City.*

release, "I insisted on not making a strict documentary, but one based on my emotional memories—a subjective essay, which I discovered after completion was my farewell to Liverpool" (Quart). But what *is* this place we see onscreen that has haunted Davies's career? The city we see in the film is postindustrial, distinguished by its slums and tenements even more than the municipal grandeur of its landmark buildings, and as memorialized by Davies it seems trapped in amber. But is this a city that hasn't moved on, or is it just Davies who is locked in a moment forever imbued with a complicated nostalgia? A borough of Merseyside, a county in Northwest England, Liverpool was once one of the major ports in Europe—in the early nineteenth century, at the height of its status as a locus of commerce, nearly a fifth of world trade went through it, and it was known as a hub in the routes of the transatlantic slave trade from Africa to the Americas. At points during this period, Liverpool was an even wealthier city than London. In the twentieth century, however, the city was wracked with enormous economic difficulties, stemming from the Great Depression in the 1930s, the destruction wrought by World War II in the 1940s, and the decline of its manufacturing and shipping industries in the 1970s. Partly as a result of its being a port city, Liverpool, home of the "Scouser" (a long-held nickname for a Liverpudlian taken from a meat stew eaten by sailors), retains a significant immigrant population, and the social makeup of the city has long been identified as among the most diverse in England—its black community, for instance, is the oldest in Great Britain, and the city is home to Europe's earliest Chinese populace. That Davies has only hinted at Liverpool's economic deprivations and social upheavals in his films, and that he has mostly ignored the city's considerable multiculturalism (an exception is one brief yet pointed scene in *The Long Day Closes*, in which a West Indian man mistakenly arrives at the family's address and is rudely, fearfully cast off), could be seen as evidence of economic and cultural myopia on his part. Yet in *Of Time and the City*, as much as in his fiction features set in Liverpool, such as *Distant Voices, Still Lives* and *The Long Day Closes*, Davies is creating an unabashedly subjective memory piece, not a social history. The Liverpool we see in *Of Time and the City* is largely white and Christian (Irish Protestant and Catholic), and it encompasses found footage of the city's streets, ports, row houses, and slums from 1945 to 1973, the years that Davies lived there. "They asked why I hadn't put certain things in the film, like the Toxteth riots. I said, 'Because it's not part of my psyche and it's not part of my emotion.' When I was growing up, Toxteth was a long way away and you just didn't go places a long way away," he told Wally Hammond in *Time Out London* in 2008.[1]

That Davies views documentary filmmaking with the same emotionality as his fiction films doesn't make his form of social anthropology any less valid. One of the most prized attributes of nonfiction film has always been its supposed objectivity—commonly a documentary will receive praise for its balance, its filmmaker's ability to view a given subject from all angles, and even its air of detachment. By being his own narrator, Davies makes dispassion all but impossible, placing his highly emotive self at the center of the film, positioning himself as its protagonist. The ever performative Davies effectively queers this most staid of nonfiction film traditions, invigorating what is often the drab, sexless omniscience of the documentary narrator with his defiantly colorful persona. This rather explicitly makes the documentary itself a performance: Davies coos and purrs and wraps his lips around his quotations from poetry and literature, honeyed reminiscences, and spiked barbs with rapturous delight; he often sounds as though he's leaning in to beckon the listener ever closer to fireside tales. Davies has pointed to a 1962 television appearance by Alec Guinness, reciting Eliot's *Four Quartets*, from memory, over the course of four nights, as one of the most influential artistic touchstones of his life. Davies's narration in *Of Time and the City*—in which *The Four Quartets* is quoted at intervals—distinctly evokes this seminal moment, identifying the film as a particularly lyrical work that is perhaps less indebted to recent nonfiction traditions than to the more unorthodox, and less commercial, characteristics of the essay film, which Timothy Corrigan describes as tending to "lean toward intellectual reflections that often insist on more conceptual or pragmatic responses, well outside the borders of conventional pleasure principles" (5).

"My template was Humphrey Jennings's *Listen to Britain*, one of the great visual poems," said Davies (qtd. in Corless, "Listen" 22), providing clues to the kind of documentary mode in which he feels most comfortable. Jennings was a photographer, painter, writer, and cofounder of the major social-research organization Mass Observation, established in 1937, in addition to a trailblazer in British documentary whose greatest works offered an aestheticized beauty as well as photorealism. His films, such as *Fires Were Started* (1941), a depiction of the working life of British firefighters, included reenactments, though this was not uncommon, as the skirting of the line between fiction and documentary was a hallmark of early documentary practice; such methods were also visible in the work of Robert Flaherty and Jennings's mentor, John Grierson, who defined documentary as "the creative treatment of actuality" (8). *Listen to Britain* (1942) was, like many of Jennings's 1940s films, made as official propaganda for the British war effort, but it is hardly reminiscent of other films produced for this purpose, which are often transparent in their aims. Set over the course of one day during the period of Germany's sustained attack on Britain known as the Blitz, *Listen to Britain* is diffuse, even ambiguous, and is structured in a nonlinear fashion, without commentary of any kind. Instead we are left to infer connections from what we see: British soldiers scanning the waterfront; a civilian dance in which the crowd sings along to "Roll Out the Barrel" (a popular song in England during the war that was based on a 1927 Czech tune); women factory workers toiling away without complaint; shots of untouched land and forest; wind whipping through tall grasses; chimney stacks silhouetted against dark gray skies; and public performances by the renowned pianist Myra Hess, the comedy-musical duo Flanagan and Allen, and a uniformed military orchestra. With its associative, rhythmic editing, *Listen to Britain* is more symphonic than didactic, creating in nineteen vivid minutes a tone poem that depicts wartime England as a resourceful, resilient, and righteous land worth saving, a place in complete harmony with itself. Using only diegetic music (each of the pieces employed to accompany montages of cityscapes and clouds originates from one of the performances shown in the film), it is defiantly unadorned propaganda. Also, in its reliance on classical and popular music to express its characters' unspoken feelings, the film is a clear progenitor of Davies's work, including *Distant Voices, Still Lives* as well as *Of Time and the City*.

In his famous essay "Only Connect: Some Aspects of the Work of Humphrey Jennings," Lindsay Anderson identified one of Jennings's great attributes as "a fascination with the commonplace thing or person that is significant precisely because it is commonplace" (89). This recalls Davies's interest in "the poetry of the ordinary, ordinary things happening to ordinary people" (qtd. in Kirkham and O'Shaugnessy 14). The architectural grandness of parts of Liverpool—teased at during passages near the opening and closing of *Of Time and the City*, the first in which the camera cranes up the dramatic façade of St. George's Hall (its bronze doors gilded with SPQL, the Roman symbol of municipal pride) accompanied by the triumphant overture for George Frideric Handel's 1749 "Music for the Royal Fireworks"; the latter with shots of fireworks exploding over the city's skyline—does not seem to capture Davies's imagination as much as the many images of the shabbier everyday lives of the working-class folks who inhabit its less regal quarters, as well as the impoverished who live in comparative squalor. One of the film's most moving passages is a wordless but emotionally effusive extended sequence that evokes those lives. Set to the Romanian soprano Angela Gheorghiu's performance of Gheorghe Popescu Branesti's "Watch and Pray," it stitches together poignant images of mundane activities enacted by working-class individuals: an elderly woman lighting a stove and warming her hands over it; a little boy getting out of bed; a girl combing her hair; a middle-aged man shaving in front of the bathroom mirror; mothers scrubbing the front stone steps and washing windows; a rag man passing on his cart; men laboring over huge bundles of wires. In pairing this otherwise unremarkable footage with Gheorghiu's prayerful song, Davies imparts a sense of contentment amidst routine and economic deprivation, a pragmatic nobility that naturally flows out of the minor details of everyday living.

Davies's reverence for the minutiae of working-class family life is evident in these scenes; it would now be helpful to chart the particulars of Davies's past to understand where this adoration comes from. Born in November 1945, Davies was the youngest of ten children, seven of whom survived infancy. Raised, as were so many of his generation and community, in a culture of strict Irish Catholicism, Davies grew up timid and God-fearing, devoted to his mother and terrified of his horrifically abusive father, who regularly beat his wife and children. The family lived in a poor section of Liverpool, where the warmth amongst their neighbors and the friends and paramours of his older siblings created a buffer against the violence of his father and instilled in him a love of community and a sense of shared struggle. His frightening home life was ameliorated after his father died of stomach cancer when Davies was only seven, finally allowing his house to be a place of refuge for the boy. "Eighteen Kensington Street is my home, and that'll never change, because that's where I was happiest," Davies said in an online interview. "Well, for four years anyway, between the death of my father in '52 to the moment I went to secondary school in '56, those were wonderful years"

(Concannon). The sense of joy one gets from his films, the personal pull to an earlier era, is attributable to this period, which Davies speaks of to this day with jovial fondness and bonhomie, poring over every concrete detail of domestic life with relish. The great emotional paradox of his career starts here.

These halcyon days—depicted as a dream world only occasionally punctured by nightmares in *The Long Day Closes*—were defined by Davies's love of popular music, especially American, and movies, both British comedies such as Robert Hamer's *Kind Hearts and Coronets* (1949) and Frank Launder's *The Happiest Days of Your Life* (1950), and more extravagant Hollywood spectacles like Stanley Donen and Gene Kelly's Technicolor musical *Singin' in the Rain* (1952) and Henry Koster's biblical epic *The Robe* (1953), the first film ever shot in the widescreen Cinemascope format. The movies were nearly a religion for Davies: "You went to school, you went to church, if you were Catholic, you went to the movies—and there were eight within walking distance of my house" (Concannon). School and church, however, could not offer as much succor as did the cinema—doing nothing to alleviate the pain of his growing awareness of his homosexuality, school and church replaced his dead father as symbols of tyrannical patriarchy and made his teenage years a time of great anguish. Once he was pried from the maternal embrace of his Catholic primary school and moved to the more oppressively masculine environment of the inner-city Sacred Heart Roman Catholic Boys' School, he found himself pitted against both uncaring authority figures and violent bullies, who immediately sensed the outsider status of this pale, reserved, decidedly *un*masculine child. When he was fifteen, Davies left school to work as a clerk in a shipping office, followed by an accounting apprenticeship, experiences that allowed him to get away from the abuse heaped upon him at school, but which he nevertheless found drab and depressing. As for religion, Davies would grow increasingly tortured over his supposed savior's inability to quell his anguish over his own sexual desires. According to Davies, "The seven years from fifteen to twenty-two were awful, and I never ever want to go through anything like that again" (Concannon).

Davies's response was to finally leave behind the sources of his anxiety and disillusionment, even though it also meant his first steps away from the home life he viewed in many ways with reverence. At age twenty-two, he decided Catholicism was a lie and walked out of church during the offertory part of Mass and never came back. As for his artistic career, it would not flower until the 1970s. Once he had left school at age fifteen, Davies, bristling with a creative urge, had found an emotional and artistic outlet acting with amateur theater companies in Liverpool ("My sisters had encouraged me from when I was seven or eight to dance and sing with them, so now I really wanted to act" [Dixon 188]). This experience ultimately led to his being awarded a Local Education Authority grant in 1972 to study at the Coventry Drama School, an educational environment he ultimately found exclusionary and closed-minded. It was at this time that he decided, on a whim after hearing about the BFI Production Board on BBC Radio, to make a short film. He sent his script, *Children*, to the BFI, who awarded him 8,500 pounds to shoot it—a daunting challenge, considering that Davies had never been on a movie set, let alone directed a film. Despite the fact that Davies claims he was not made to feel comfortable on set by his crew ("It was really the most unpleasant three weeks, to be told every day that it's lousy," he told me in interview), he would go on to make two more shorts that along with *Children* would compose his *Trilogy*: *Madonna and Child*, completed in 1980 after he had become a student at the National Film School in London, and *Death and Transfiguration*, which he directed in 1983 after graduation, made with financing from the BFI and the Greater London Arts Association.

Taken together, these three short films assume a single narrative, charting the physical growth, disillusionment, and eventual decay of Tucker from traumatized boy to stunted middle-aged man to elderly nursing-home patient haunted by the inescapable events of his past and crippled by religious guilt and homosexual shame. Though as a whole the films move ahead in such a way that Tucker's progression from child to geriatric is clearly defined, the *Trilogy* rejects linearity. Each installment in the triptych uses a diffuse present as a focal point, only to jump ahead and back in time, resulting in a film that feels like it's not existing at any set historical point but is rather made up of a constant negotiation between past, present, and future, unbound to anything other than its protagonist's (and by extension its maker's) psyche. Therefore, Davies was already experimenting with film's very form—with what Gilles Deleuze calls the "time-image," an interpenetration of past and future in one "present" moment that is more virtual than real—as he was simultaneously learning its basic technical craft.

Like the *Trilogy*, *Distant Voices, Still Lives* unexpectedly grew into a feature out of circumstance. As reflected in its bifurcated title, it is split into two discrete narratives, approximately forty minutes each. Davies originally intended only to produce the first part, *Distant Voices*, concerning the emotionally crippling effects of a patriarch's abuse on his wife and children, told in a dramatically nonlinear fashion, hopping around in a somber dance of free association. But after a successful preview screening at the National Film Theater in London and subsequent enthusiasm from its BFI and Channel 4 producers, who felt that the film had potential to reach wide audiences, Davies was encouraged to promote it to feature length. With a major budget increase, this resulted in a second half, *Still Lives*, which picks up with the same characters— Mother and her three grown children, Eileen, Maisie, and Tony—years after the death of their father, whose presence still hangs over their every interaction like a pale ghost in wait. Shot two years after *Distant Voices*, this sequel of sorts eloquently evokes the passage of time, by virtue of the noticeably aged faces and bodies of the actors onscreen as well as by the manner in which Davies constructs and visualizes it like a haunted echo of the first film. Together, they create an arresting, kaleidoscopic portrait of one family's history, a "pattern of timeless moments," as Davies has called it (*Modest Pageant* 74), quoting the last of Eliot's *Four Quartets*, "Little Gidding."

His next film, *The Long Day Closes*, was a more direct reckoning with the self. Its protagonist, Bud—tantalized, to his great shame, by bare male flesh; terrorized by tyrannical teachers waving rulers; perplexed by religion; devoted to his caring mother; and unabashedly delighted by Hollywood movies—is fictionalized but unmistakably the director (Davies's childhood nickname was, in fact, Bud). *The Long Day Closes* takes place in the late 1950s, a period of relative tranquility following the death of Bud's father, who is never seen or spoken of onscreen. Yet his absence gives the film an odd free-floating tension: *The Long Day Closes* becomes a film whose only true villain is an unsure future. The central dramatic irony—here, a decidedly queer one, in formal and autobiographical terms—is that we're watching a paradise we know will soon be lost. It is a meditation on the erosion of youth that plays out as a cubist idyll.

Davies's autobiographical impulse was intense from the beginning. He said in 1988, "I make films in order to come to terms with my family history" (qtd. in Houston 174). According to T. S. Eliot in "Little Gidding": "This is the use of memory / For liberation—not less of love but expanding / of love beyond desire, and so liberation / From the future as well as the past." In a sense, Davies's entire career is a way of negotiating the nostalgia he clearly feels for his childhood with the trauma that defined it. The term "trauma"—which originates as the word for a surgical wound, a rupture in the outermost layer of an organism that nevertheless causes extreme internal damage—was defined by Sigmund Freud not as an event that causes constant rupture "but its delayed revival as a *memory* after the individual had entered sexual maturity and had grasped its sexual meaning," as Ruth Leys explains (20). Leys also points to Freud's 1899 study "Screen Memories," which might seem particularly relevant to our purposes, as it "concludes by questioning 'whether we have any memories at all *from* our childhood: memories *relating to* our childhood may be all that we possess'" (20–21). To the first point, we can locate Davies's emergence as an artist using the cinematic medium to "come to terms" with his past during the same basic span of time that he was coming to terms with his own sexuality. Looked at this way, the nonlinearity of the films in the *Trilogy*, *Distant Voices, Still Lives*, and *The Long Day Closes* is expressive of the Freudian notion of the return of the repressed, delineating the events of Davies's childhood by having them surface a bit at a time, bubbling up from a dark chasm as perhaps unwanted recollections, which also helps explain the dreamlike logic on which much of his work functions. In "Screen Memories," Freud writes, "No one doubts that our earliest childhood experiences have left indelible traces on our inner selves; but when we question our *memory* as to what impressions are destined to influence us till the end of our lives, it comes up with either nothing at all or a relatively small number of isolated recollections, often of questionable or perplexing significance" (3). Freud's notion that our memories are inherently untrustworthy because of the unstable nature of the human mind is also illustrative of a key conundrum of Davies's work: that autobiography is completely subjective, and only through a fictionalizing of the past can one begin to fully grasp its truths.

There are three loci of trauma from Davies's childhood that represent the events with which he must "come to terms" throughout his films: (a) institutional suffering, typified by the emotional misuse he endured at church and school, dramatized in *The Long Day Closes* as twinned patriarchal spaces that filled the void left by his father's death; (b) family, specifically the abuse of his father and its detrimental effects on himself, his siblings, and his mother; and (c) sexuality, meaning Davies's feelings about his own gay desires, a discomfort fostered in adolescence that continued into his adulthood and middle age. The negative emotional repercussions of all three sites of trauma can be felt in his films. In this sense, Davies's work paints its artist as one driven by masochism. Tony Williams writes that "Davies's films depict a masochistic realm of unpleasure rather than pleasure, a situation due to patriarchal oppression" (247). Although his statements that he makes films to exorcise his demons would seem to point to some sort of positive outcome from delving into all this pain, Davies has claimed to have found no epiphany, stating in a 2008 online interview, "I thought at one time, when I started making my films, particularly the early autobiographical ones, that I would reach some catharses. But I haven't. All it has done is highlight that which has been lost" (Hillis).

School and Church

Davies began his filmmaking career with a depiction of institutionally wrought suffering that could not be taken as anything other than deeply personal and profoundly uncomfortable—indeed, *Children* is his most explicitly morose film about youth, and one that announces Davies's perspective as a gay filmmaker. Robert Tucker, introduced as an adolescent in *Children* (he is identified in Davies's screenplay as fifteen but is played by a slightly younger boy) and followed through to middle age and finally old age and death in the second and third parts of the *Trilogy*, remains Davies's most vivid, and most troublingly queer, surrogate. In these stark works—tellingly the director's only black-and-white films, with the exception of much of the found footage used in *Of Time and the City*—Tucker is allowed no moments of uncomplicated pleasure or elation. He is depicted as on a slow trajectory toward a lonely death; the film plays as one long continuum of mourning and self-hatred. As *Children* begins, we hear the sounds of young boys playing, yet these are not joyful noises; they are shouts and taunts of the schoolyard, which we first see in a high-angle shot. We are then given a close-up of Tucker's despondent face: this willowy blond boy's immobile, slack-jawed expression of dejection is one we will grow accustomed to. Here, Tucker is in the midst of being humiliated and beaten by a trio of taller, clearly stronger kids. "If you snitch we'll get you tonight," are the last words we hear before the film's title is superimposed on an image of Tucker bending over with his head between his knees. Just a few minutes into the film, and Davies has painted Tucker, and by extension himself, as an outsider, one whose youth is a locus of trauma. The film's dramatic, monolithic title imparts a grand statement of intent, implying that this is not only an expression of Tucker's childhood but of childhood itself, a time of life beset by doubt and terror.

The fear instilled in Tucker by the bullies is paralleled a few scenes later in the authoritarian punishment meted out by the headmaster, who sadistically canes the left hands of Tucker and one of the bullies with whom he is caught fighting in the hallway. The torment of school radiates from both Tucker's peers and elders; we do not witness him conversing with anyone who might be considered a friend, nor do we see him engaged in any enriching learning experience. His classmates and superiors are equally power-tripping, offering no comfort for Tucker, existing only to reestablish a patriarchal world of abuse and domination outside of the home. This notion of educational institutions being nerve centers of systematic dehumanization is explored even further as it relates to Davies's other most sharply defined surrogate character, Bud, in *The Long Day Closes*, which repeats *Children*'s images of bullying ("Who's a fruit, then?" is a schoolyard taunt directed at both Tucker and Bud) and authoritarian discipline: the headmaster in *The Long Day Closes* shows an almost gleeful predilection for caning boys' hands, evidenced by the way he eagerly rises from his desk to whip Bud, squeezing his rod in anticipation, for the minor infraction of tardiness.

The ways in which the educational environment doubles as a site of profound humiliation for Bud are not tied exclusively to acts of corporal punishment and reprimanding. Davies paints the entire secondary-school experience as one of intimidation and bewilderment. This had not been the case with Bud's (and Davies's) years at his primary Catholic school, run by nuns depicted in the film as warmly maternal. In an early sequence, Bud, plagued by a persistent bloody nose, is allowed to stay in the headmistresses' office until the hemorrhage subsides. In the shot, Bud sits in the foreground in profile, while the headmistress faces the camera at the center of the frame. As Bud waits, the camera tracks in slowly on the nun as she patiently writes at her desk, and then there is a dissolve to a shot that tracks backwards and out of the office through a window. The room is now empty, as though already a distant memory rather than a concrete place in time. With another dissolve Davies unceremoniously transitions to the secondary school, immediately signified by an instance of schoolyard bullying, and then by the masculine swagger of its educators. Mr. Nicholls introduces himself to his new students by giving them sharp thwacks across their hands simply to prove who's in charge ("You play ball with me, I'll play ball with you"). This oppressive school is thus identified as the provenance of the paternal, marking a distinct contrast to the mother-identified, more womblike space of Bud's primary education. This was the intention of the production designer Christopher Hobbs, who "made Bud's primary school a place of coziness and warmth . . . while the 'big' school to which he moves, where he is unhappy, beaten, and humiliated, is cold, sparse, and empty" (Kirkham and O'Shaughnessy 13). That this sequence is directly preceded by Bud's mother musing in voiceover, "I wonder what 1956 will bring" (following a spirited New Year's Eve celebration), further intimates the importance of this transition for Bud, identifying it as a clear break from a happy time—one blissfully untouched by the dominance of a father or father figure—to one infected by anxiety and violence.

The split between caring women and intimidating men is complicated, however, by the presence of the school's puckered nurse, a middle-aged reptile who calmly yet coldly scans the boys' hair for lice, and later in the film sneers to Bud when he reports for an ear infection, "What nasty little creatures you boys are." The nurse seems to represent a certain perversity—a woman drained of maternal instinct. Bud's face seems to absorb her humiliation with the same terrified stoicism with which he greets the world's many confusions. In this case, Davies's decision to hold on Bud's face while she professes her disgust at him intimates his internalization of her words, which can only exacerbate the shame Bud already feels for his own body. It is clear from a moment in which Bud delays exiting a changing room at the school gymnasium's pool that he too believes himself to be a "nasty little creature."

The shame Davies was made to feel about himself sprung from religion as well as school. "The church did me a great deal of damage," Davies has claimed. "For somebody like me, who discovered at puberty that they were gay (it was then a criminal offense in Britain), the church offered no succor. I felt then that if I prayed and was really good, God would make me like everybody else. Those years when I prayed until my knees bled were awful" (Quart). The anger Davies feels about his own religious upbringing surfaces as ambivalence in the *Trilogy* and *The Long Day Closes* (some of their most shocking imagery mingles sexual desire and religious iconography, which I will later examine), but as something more vicious and strange in *The Neon Bible*, a work embedded in a culture informed by a Protestant sect depicted as particularly narrow-minded. The film feels at times intensely personal in its take on the influence of the church on the lives of the vulnerable, though its milieu and specific religious denomination are distinct from the Catholicism agonizingly depicted in Davies's more directly autobiographical films.

John Kennedy Toole, the author of the novel on which *The Neon Bible* is based, was, like Davies, skeptical about Christianity, though in his case it was specifically the Calvinist religions of the American South where he was raised. Written when the New Orleans–bred Toole (best known for his far more stylized second novel, *A Confederacy of Dunces*, which posthumously earned him a Pulitzer Prize) was only sixteen, *The Neon Bible* is hardly a tract against religion, although it is distinguished by its highly critical take on religious fundamentalism, particularly in the Calvinist Baptist community of the 1930s and 1940s. Nor is it considered a work of autobiography: though it takes the form of a first-person coming-of-age narrative—that of young, melancholy David—it is a largely fanciful story Toole conceived while visiting relatives in rural Mississippi, an area he observed as oppressive due to its socially ingrained religious bigotry. Coming only a few years after *The Long Day Closes*, which Davies claimed in 1992 would be the last of his autobiographical films (Dixon 193), *The Neon Bible* represents Davies's initial attempt at adapting someone else's material. But perhaps most importantly, it also marks the realization of his first story told in a largely linear fashion. While *The Neon Bible* is for all intents and purposes a cause-and-effect narrative, Davies complicates matters by refusing to make explicit the connections between events; although the film does progress forward, it constantly feels held back by an aesthetic stasis, a matter that I'll return to later. The film is thus an example of how an unorthodox aesthetic subtly changes the tenor and identity of a preexisting text. Davies himself has somewhat disavowed the film, citing it as more of a stepping-stone project than a success in its own right ("I think it was a transitional work, because it came mostly from the book and yet it was a bit autobiographical, too," he told Graham Fuller in *Film Comment* in 2001 ["Summer's End" 55]).

But, despite the negative notices and an outright hostile reaction from the notoriously vociferous crowds at the Cannes Film Festival, where it met with boos and catcalls (Coe 12), *The Neon Bible* achieves an extraordinary tonal and ideological coherence, noticed by some critics, particularly Jonathan Rosenbaum in an April 5, 1996, *Chicago Reader* review: "*The Neon Bible* may not qualify as a masterpiece, as *Distant Voices, Still Lives* and *The Long Day Closes* do, but it still contains moments and achievements that are as impressive as anything Davies has ever done—and to have done this with alien material makes his achievement even more remarkable."

The odd aesthetic determinism of Davies's film might be attributable to his outsider status as a working-class British director exploring the eccentricities and small-mindedness perceived by Toole in the American Bible Belt. The stylized detachment of the film—shots held long past the point of comfort; scenes set up as rich tableaux that appear more artificial than naturalistic; musical interludes reminiscent of those on *Distant Voices, Still Lives* and *The Long Day Closes*, which here take the audience out of the film rather than immerse them in it—creates a necessary distancing layer between the material and its maker, almost an admission by Davies that he's a fish out of water, as well as further establishes the artistic differences between his work, which aims for a poetic unity, and Toole's, which is straightforward, unmannered prose, marked by sharp, staccato sentences. Yet *The Neon Bible*'s depiction of the occasionally insidious effects of organized religion, specifically on young David, is direct and powerful, especially in Davies's divergences from Toole's text.

The Neon Bible follows David from preadolescence to his late teenage years, during which he must contend with an abusive father (Denis Leary); a caring but mentally ill and ineffectual mother (Diana Scarwid); the gradual disillusionment he feels toward his beloved and exotic Aunt Mae (Gena Rowlands); the pain and loss wrought by World War II, from which his drafted father never returns; and the intense dislocation he perceives as a result of the conservative and prejudiced religious community in which he lives. All of these are acutely felt, but dramatized in diffuse, almost abstract ways, so *The Neon Bible* becomes a film of internalized emotion and mood rather than literal cause and effect, placing it in the realm of dream logic (an evocation, again, of Freud's return of the repressed) instead of character study. In an arrestingly imagined scene, Davies takes us inside the tent revival of the traveling evangelical preacher Bobbie Lee Taylor, who has come down from Tennessee. This is a major event in the book and the film, though Davies's visualization of Toole's chapter transforms it into something grander, stranger, and wholly cinematic, not to mention strikingly personal. Toole provides much buildup to the evangelist's arrival, charting the proliferating signs around town advertising the revival, and describing the anticipation and excitement surging through the citizenry about his imminent visit. When the day finally comes for David, his mother, and Aunt Mae to attend the performance, we have been properly prepared, and Toole lets Bobbie Lee fly off on a seven-page rant about social degradation and licentiousness ("Today our nation is having a mortal struggle with the devil. In camps young girls are dancing with sailors and soldiers, and who knows what-all . . ." [68]). Davies, however, allows no anticipation, literally dropping us into the world of Bobbie Lee Taylor without warning. Following a beautiful, expansive image of the starry night sky, Davies's camera cranes down to reveal a banner announcing the preacher's show and then proceeds to follow swarms of townsfolk as they walk in clusters down a main commercial street, moving with purpose. After a dissolve, the camera glides ahead of them and enters the revival tent, which ominously glows and flickers from inside, a candle-strewn temple of doom. As the audience members begin to take their seats, Davies cuts to Bobbie Lee (Leo Burmester), who stands backstage, watching the crowd while eerily mouthing along to a prerecorded self-introduction (in the book, an older, suited man does the honors of heralding the preacher's entrance). Davies's establishment of Bobbie Lee as less man of God than a man behind the curtain immediately evokes the charlatan title character of *The Wizard of Oz*. Toole casts a disbelieving eye on Bobbie Lee, but Davies leaves little space to consider him as anything but a fraud, connecting *The Neon Bible* explicitly to the director's identity as a lapsed Christian who views the religion as a lie.

An even more visually daring evocation of religious skepticism and dread can be seen late in *The Long Day Closes*. In a frightening daydream envisioned while he kneels next to his mother at church, Bud imagines Christ's crucifixion. The camera begins trained on the right hand as it is being nailed to the cross, and then proceeds to dolly up and over his body, so that we're looking straight down at the stretched figure. All else in the room is obscured by complete darkness, so the crucifixion appears to be occurring in a void; meanwhile, a prevalent echoey creaking on the sound track lends the scene a sense of interiority, as though the death is happening inside a private space. (The noise was a happy accident, according to the filmmakers, due to the weight of the camera and equipment involved; this extraordinarily complicated shot took nine hours to set up and shoot, as Davies reports in the introduction to his book of screenplays, *A Modest Pageant* [xii].) When we are directly suspended above this image, the Christ figure abruptly raises his head, looks into the camera, and breaks the silence by screaming at Bud in a shocking outburst; his "terrifying human bark," as Davies describes it in his original script, sounds a lot like Bud's name. The eagle-eyed viewer will recognize, in this brief flash, that this actor (Kirk McLaughlin), naked except for a loincloth, is the same one who plays the muscular bricklayer who arouses Bud earlier in the film. Thus this image of Jesus is a perplexing and, to Bud, damning fantasy that awakens his desire as well as his fears.

Perplexing religion in *The Neon Bible* and *The Long Day Closes.*

The Sins of the Father

The centrality of religion in Davies's life was a by-product of cultural expectation more than any extraordinary piety on the part of his family. Davies's family enjoyed the hallmarks of a secular existence steeped in popular culture, including music and movies, fashion, and pub-crawling. Davies's decision to cinematically celebrate his family's personal joys while at the same time exorcising the demons surrounding them, a process most explicit in *Distant Voices, Still Lives,* infers the queer paradoxes in his work. A personal-memory film in which Davies has excluded himself from the narrative, *Distant Voices, Still Lives* is the director's most complicated work of autobiography. The film's three main characters—sisters Eileen (Angela Walsh) and Maisie (Lorraine Ashbourne), and brother Tony (Dean Williams)—are based on three of Davies's siblings, yet they unavoidably stand in for all of them, and their experiences of the abuse and pain that their father (Pete Postlethwaite) inflicted upon them and their mother (Freda Dowie) forms the heart of a crisscrossing narrative of Davies's family. The highly stylized tactics of the film disallow any reading of strict realism, however. Even its location is unclear: "The setting is deliberately denied a geographical specificity . . . the film does not have a Liverpool accent. It is a work of intense interiority, unmediated by the particularity of the place" (Wilson 282).

Especially in the bifurcation between *Distant Voices* and *Still Lives*, separate films shot two years apart with subtly variant rhythms, the overall work has a sense of at once being there and being nowhere. It is both a film of intense subjectivity and heightened dissociation, the latter caused by narrative leaps between different times and spaces and the complex use of tracking shots and single takes. It is also a film about presence and absence, specifically that of the father, who is seen in the flesh only in *Distant Voices*; set years later, *Still Lives* takes place after he has died from cancer, and although he is effectively gone from the narrative proper—warranting barely a passing reference—he nevertheless presides over it, quite literally in the shot in which a framed photograph of him (a photograph of Davies's actual father) hangs behind an otherwise peaceful image of the mother perched on her reading chair. *Distant Voices, Still Lives* is a work of dreamlike subjectivity minus the perspective of a main character; without a Davies surrogate like Tucker or Bud, there is a purposeful hole at its center. This lack of a stabilizing point of view easily allows for its freeform experiments in narrative, its transformation of autobiography into a work of unsettling nonlinearity. Tony Williams argues that, "By identifying himself with the camera instead of a surrogate figure, Davies more acutely explores the familial situation" (244). Davies's disinterest in isolating family members and following them for any extended period of time, preferring instead to hop from one to the next in stream-of-conscious associations, gives his family portrait an intimacy, making the audience feel as though it is privy not to events but to innermost fears, dreams, desires, secrets, and, of course, memories.

However, despite the abstract nature of the film's form, most of the scenes in *Distant Voices, Still Lives*, as in *Children* and *The Long Day Closes*, are versions of events that did happen in Davies's family, whether taken from his own memory or as related to him by siblings. According to Davies in a 2012 online interview with *The Guardian*, "When you're the youngest of ten, you don't see events fully, you just feel intense moments. And life was extreme—either ecstatically happy or utterly miserable. I was seven when my dad died, but afterwards my family would talk about what happened when he was alive. Those memories almost became mine, they were so vivid" (Abbott). In keeping with how Davies remembers his childhood, these moments in the film toggle back and forth between the "happy" and the "miserable." After Mother and the three siblings are introduced at the opening of the film, looking directly into the camera in a static tableau that lends the motion-picture frame the feel of a faded photograph (although Davies claims that his family did not own a camera and thus this aesthetic was not dictated by a specific reality), we are soon made aware of the one character missing from the group when Eileen says out loud, "I wish me Dad was here." Her sister, Maisie, responds, but in voiceover that only we are privileged to hear: "I don't . . . he was a bastard and I bleedin' hated him." This leads directly to a subjective flashback of Maisie on all fours, scrubbing the basement floor, asking her father permission to go to a dance; he stands over her, proceeds to throw change at her, and then beats her viciously with a broom handle. Though we see the father raising and lowering the household weapon again and again, Davies keeps Maisie out of frame, and we only hear her screams rather than see the blows being rained down on her. Davies also elides onscreen violence in the film's next disturbing moment of recall, which belongs to brother Tony, whom we see smashing their house's front window with bare, bleeding fists, screaming in an angry yet fearful and melancholy wail, presumably to his father, "Come out and fight, you bastard!" The instigation for and result of the incident are never revealed, painting the moment as both specific—a vivid memory of a particular time and place—and standing in for an ongoing, systematic series of confrontations between father and son that has clearly defined their combative and resentful relationship.

Despite the economy with which it is depicted, the paternal violence in the film is among cinema's most jarring depictions of abuse, especially for the manner in which it tends to erupt unexpectedly. At one point, Davies seems to be divulging a surprisingly fond memory related to his father during an idyllic Christmas flashback. After Davies dreamily shows the family decorating its modest tree, the holiday hymn "In the Bleak Midwinter" drifting across the sound track, he cuts to the children nestled snugly in their beds. They are angelic, and younger than we've seen them in any prior scene; their father enters, careful not to disturb them as he ties their Christmas stockings onto the foot of the bed. His eyes are filled with tears as he murmurs, "God bless, kids." Davies then cuts from this hushed, almost redemptive moment to a shot of the family sitting around the dining-room table for a Christmas meal. One might assume it to be the next morning, except that the children look slightly older. This time, the father, quietly quivering, appears to be on the verge of a psychotic rage. The explosion comes when he pulls the tablecloth off of the table, sending the elaborate holiday meal to the floor, rising, and screaming to the offscreen mother to clean up the mess.

The most explicit instance of onscreen physical violence in *Distant Voices*—in which Father mercilessly beats Mother in the house's hallway—is complicated by the use of tonal counterpoint. First we see Mother perched precariously on a ledge on the house's second floor washing windows, a dangerous position that causes young Maisie, watching from below, to murmur, "Please don't fall, Mum." Ella Fitzgerald's major-key, up-tempo "Taking a Chance on Love" drifts across the sound track. At first, the memory seems largely pleasant—the child's reminiscence of the mother doing household chores is one necessarily filled with nostalgia—but the sense of jeopardy created by her being on the ledge leads to an image of her in true danger, this time at the brutal hands of the father. It's as though the mind of the filmmaker is working spontaneously while we watch, given to uncontrollable divergences, slippages, and neuroses. The song places the horror of the moment within a continuum of joy and misery, expressing that for Davies, memory is an ever-flowing process, and a poignant recollection often leads directly to a dreadful one. Fitzgerald sings of the risks involved in giving yourself up to romance ("Here I go again / I hear those trumpets blow again / All aglow again / Taking a chance on love"), and the ironic juxtaposition—between the fantasy of love and a reality of misery—creates something unspeakably painful.

It is worth pointing out that the re-creation of this particular remembrance in *Distant Voices* was too traumatic for the filmmaker, who was not present on the set when it was shot, as recalled by the actress Freda Dowie in 2012 (Abbott). At moments like these, the real trumps the imaginary for Davies. "I don't want to watch violence. I had enough of that in my childhood," he said to me in interview. For all the traumas bubbling beneath them, Davies's films largely abstain from explicit depictions of violence. *The Neon Bible* features two major exceptions, both included in fidelity to the source material: the first when the father shockingly punches the mother in the face after she criticizes him for spending what little money they have on seeds for his garden, and the second at the film's disorienting climax. In the peculiar penultimate chapter of Toole's novel, David arrives home to find his perpetually sickly mother dying in a pool of her own blood, the cause unclear. When the local preacher—a man whom David has inherently distrusted for his self-righteous piety—arrives for the purpose of taking his mother, who had become increasingly mentally unhinged, to an asylum, David refuses to divulge her whereabouts; after the preacher ascends the stairs to find her, David proceeds to shoot him in the back of the head with his father's gun. Davies faithfully dramatizes this sudden and unexpected killing, which effectively recalibrates the entire narrative, all of which had been related as flashback from a later point in time, when David was escaping town on a train heading north. It now becomes clear that he has been running away not only from his past but also from his own murderous act. The events happen as abruptly in Davies's film as in Toole's novel, though Davies visualizes them without Toole's first-person immediacy. In a dispassionate single take, with the staircase in the background of the shot, David accomplishes the bloody deed; Davies responds to the act by slowly tracking in on the preacher's lifeless body, its hand ominously pointing straight down—the camera maintains a gingerly, hesitant, even courteous, distance.

Viewing *The Neon Bible* in personal terms for its director, the murder of the preacher would seem to symbolize the deaths of two important figures in Davies's life. He could be seen to represent the absent father, who has returned to claim the body of the mother, and as a "man of God" he also stands in for the uncaring church, unable to provide help or spiritual guidance unless it is self-serving. The eradication of these twin patriarchal symbols forces David out of his home and into the great unknown, an act of both hope and of loss. In an inescapably Freudian vein, however, the death of the father heralds the beginning rather than precipitates the end of many of Davies's films, including *Madonna and Child*; *Still Lives*, which flashes forward to the late 1950s, following the early to middle years of the decade depicted in *Distant Voices*; and *The Long Day Closes*. *Children* climaxes with the funeral of Tucker's father, following his painful death by stomach cancer; when *Madonna and Child* opens, it is many years later, and Tucker is middle-aged, still living with his mother, miserably unhappy at the drab office where he serves as clerk, and guilt-plagued by his sadomasochistic homosexual desires. He has moved on, but he remains emotionally stunted. *Still Lives*, bookended by the birth of Maisie's first child and Tony's wedding, takes place largely during one extended pub visit; all of it is haunted by the absence of the father, of whom the film makes not a whisper. The father is also never mentioned in the entirety of *The Long Day Closes*. Yet in one scene, he is clearly invoked: Bud has a nightmare in which two rough, masculine hands lunge out of the pitch dark surrounding his bed and grab him by the head. Bud wakes up screaming, "It was a *man*! It was a *man*!" This is perhaps the most explicit example in all of Davies's cinema of the trauma visited upon a character based on a violent history—the past is literally reaching out to haunt Bud, or at least to hold him in place. Immobilization is key to Davies's films, a by-product of his complicated relationship to nostalgia. In this image we get a literalization of the terror of being captured and bound to a traumatic memory, yet it sits alongside many fond recollections as well. As we'll see, this intimates a peculiarly queer reckoning with the past in which an undeniably, even violently, repressive era—in personal and sociopolitical terms—is remembered with an incongruous wistfulness.

Dark Desires

Perhaps the most immobilizing of Davies's traumas, and the most defining, is his sexuality. In a 2011 interview with Donald Clarke for the *Irish Times* online, he said, at age sixty-six, "Being gay has ruined my life. I hate it. I'll go to my grave hating it." The seeds of confusion and terror wrought by a burgeoning awareness of his desire for the same sex are strewn throughout three of his memory films—*Children, The Long Day*

Closes, and *Of Time and the City*—while his greatest harbored fears in relation to his homosexuality, and its perceived sinfulness and consequent loneliness, find predictive outlet in *Madonna and Child* and *Death and Transfiguration*. In all cases, homosexuality is linked to shame, a politically incorrect and dated perspective in an era in which gayness has been recouped as a marker of identity to be worn with pride. Nevertheless, it is crucial to Davies's persona and artistic perspective to acknowledge his outsider status—socially and within the film industry—which also helps us understand the connection he feels with socially outcast female characters in his novel adaptations, such as Aunt Mae in *The Neon Bible*, Lily Bart in *The House of Mirth*, and Hester in *The Deep Blue Sea*, all of whom stand as potential figures of queer identification.

The first explicitly gay moment in Davies's cinema occurs in an early and sexually forthright scene in *Children*. While showering at a public pool, pubescent Tucker finds himself fascinated by a young man with a well-developed physique who washes in front of him. The camera takes on the boy's point of view, panning down the man's body, fixing on his small swimming briefs as he puts his hand down the front of them to wash his genitals; despite Tucker's shame, the gaze is unabashedly erotic, inviting the spectator to join the boy in the realization of his pleasure. Davies zooms in on the child's face as he watches wordlessly, dumbstruck (the original screenplay, which included an ultimately deleted voiceover narration, features Tucker whispering to himself, "Look at his muscles!" [*Modest Pageant* 11]). Clarifying this scene not simply as sensual but rather as a source of trauma, Davies cuts to a haunted-looking Tucker at age twenty-four (Robin Hooper) in a psychiatrist's office. After writing a prescription for depression pills, his doctor asks Tucker, "Still no interest in girls? Well, that may come."

The entire sequence is paralleled in an early scene in *The Long Day Closes*. Bud, who has begged his mother to let him go the pictures but has instead been enlisted to help with her laundry, is perched at the back window of his row house. His mother works below, clothespinning the wash to the line; meanwhile Bud, center frame, stares straight ahead into a neighbor's backyard, in which a group of laborers are working under the hot sun to build a brick wall. Bud, intrigued by the sight of these men, especially one standing in front, muscular and stripped to the waist, watches heedlessly. The man catches his eye and winks. When

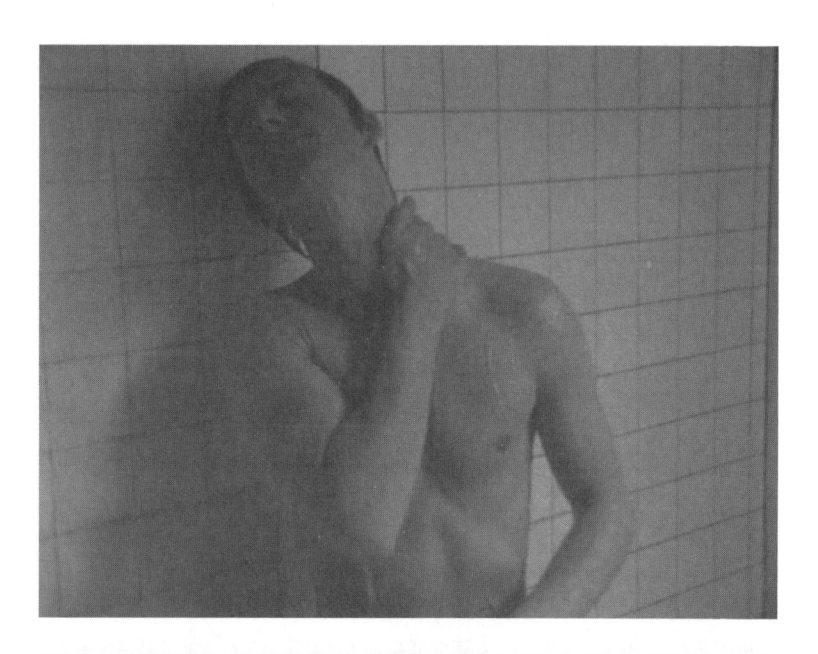

Oblivious objects of desire in *Children*
and *The Long Day Closes*.

Davies cuts back to Bud, we hear the men laughing offscreen; the boy's expression alters to bewilderment and shame as he slowly slinks into the darkness behind him. The laborer and *Children*'s man in the shower are similarly seductive figures, objects of eroticism (with matching slim-to-muscular physiques) indifferent to the gaze of their pubescent admirers,

44 | **Terence Davies**

unintentional exhibitionists whose very comfort with their own bodies forms a striking, unsettling contrast to the bodily shame they inspire in the one who is watching.

To better comprehend the revulsion Tucker and Bud feel at the moments of their sexual awakenings, it is helpful to put Davies's feelings of adolescent self-loathing in the context of England's cultural attitudes toward homosexuality in the late 1950s and early 1960s. The historical public disapproval of sex between consenting adults of the same gender—seen largely as aberrant or, worse, a "perversion"—was still widely pervasive throughout Davies's childhood, although a number of events in the 1950s brought the taboo subject out of the closet. Making homosexuality a topic of discussion also would have made Davies, along with other gay children coming of age at the time, more aware of the general disgust the notion raised in many people. Lord Edward Montagu, a young baron and politician of repute, became notorious when in 1953 and 1954 he was twice arrested and imprisoned for engaging in lewd conduct with males, many of whom were also of wealth and renowned lineage. The legendary stage and screen actor John Gielgud was likewise arrested in 1953 for attempting to pick up a man in a public restroom. These and other examples of commonly reported arrests and convictions were part of a wide governmental crackdown—escalated by the newly appointed police commissioner John Nott-Bower—on homosexuals, who were increasingly linked in the era's Communist witch-hunts, tagged as security risks in governmental jobs, and stigmatized as sexual predators. The more liberal public scrutiny over this ongoing cultural purge eventually resulted in the 1957 Wolfenden Report, which recommended legislation to legalize homosexual behavior, criminalized since an 1885 Act of Parliament. Written by a committee of fifteen members, including clergymen, politicians, academics, and doctors, the report concluded that homosexuality cannot be legitimately identified as a disease and that homosexual activity between consenting adults in the privacy of their own homes is not a matter for the government. Though the report received much press, it would not be until 1967 that legislation was enacted to overturn the 1885 act.

Basil Dearden's *Victim* (1961) a major cinematic response to the Wolfenden Report, would come when Davies was at the impressionable and fragile age of sixteen. Davies refers to the film in a revelatory passage in *Of Time and the City*. After a sequence in which he gushes over his love for cinema, fostered uncomplicatedly in his youth, accompanied by images of glamorous Hollywood movie stars, such as Gregory Peck, visiting Liverpool, Davies intones, "Later I saw Dirk Bogarde in *Victim* and discovered something altogether different." Regarded today as a landmark political film, *Victim* starred a major matinee idol in what was perceived as a risky role: a closeted, married barrister whose concealed homosexual past comes back to haunt him when he and other members of the underground gay community in London are targeted by a vicious homophobic blackmailer. Conceived by Dearden and his longtime producing partner Michael Relph as one of their many "social-problem films" of that era, *Victim* is a liberal message movie that, as the critic Raymond Durgnat claims, "urges the repeal of a law" (63). So despite its kid-gloves approach to the material (its buttoned-down air of tastefulness veers from any hint of homoeroticism) and its essentially conservative and tragic representation of the gay community, the majority of whose members are portrayed as burdened, sad-sack figures, *Victim* is nevertheless a radical and highly political film. The fact that it features a sympathetic homosexual protagonist—the first in British cinema—was no small matter, and the effect it would have had on a boy of sixteen struggling with his own homosexual feelings is incalculable. At the same time, its depiction of the gay lifestyle as one of despair and social invisibility could have proven to further frighten him; in fact, it seems to have laid the emotional groundwork for his cinematic intimations of love as tragic and doomed.

Davies's invocation of *Victim* in *Of Time and the City*—which both sets *Victim* up as an alternative to conventional Hollywood cinema and insinuates that viewing it was an altering experience for him—is followed, tellingly, by a sequence that is a more direct confessional. Over images of professional wrestling matches, Davies relates the combination of tantalization and horror he would feel watching the wrestlers in what he perceived as a hypersexualized environment, where men with immense torsos would strip to the waist and pummel one another into the ground in fits of violent ecstasy. While witnessing these sweat-and-blood-drenched behemoths, staring out from behind tight, face-obscuring rubber masks, either on television or from a stadium seat, Davies says in voiceover that he would find himself "choking with schoolboy guilt and trembling with the fear of the wrath of God." The stock images

Davies shows are more traditionally frightening than sensual, allowing him to both legitimize his sexual predilections *and* stigmatize them as somehow unwholesome.

This linkage of eroticism and violence recalls Tucker's sexual guilt in the *Trilogy*. The first suggestion of this—and one that directly connects Tucker to Davies the narrator in *Of Time and the City*, creating a clear autobiographical continuum between the films—comes in *Children*, in which we see twenty-four-year-old Tucker admiring an image collage of mostly shirtless bodybuilders and wrestlers taped to the back of his closet door. In *Death and Transfiguration*, such images have been transplanted into a photo album that the middle-aged Tucker keeps hidden away and occasionally flips through, its many pages implying that the appeal of the rugged, violent, über-masculine ideal has only increased over the years, now also incorporating bikers and other men fitted out in leather gear. Tucker's attraction to such physical types forces him to feel further social marginalization, even if such an aesthetic sexual preference is common and is interpreted as a response to a culture that has traditionally feminized gay men. The visual appeal of men in motorcycle jackets, leather caps and harnesses, sailor suits, police uniforms, wrestling outfits, and the like—all traditionally signifiers of dominant, patriarchal masculinity—has been frequently represented in art in the second half of the twentieth century, most famously in the work of the filmmaker Kenneth Anger, and controversially in the photography of Robert Mapplethorpe and the illustrations of Tom of Finland. Once considered deviant, such types have grown relatively mainstream in gay iconography, but for Tucker and Davies such aesthetic pleasures are necessarily viewed as abnormal. Here, Davies offers a productive, rather than merely retrograde, image of gay shame, a reminder of the self-loathing that persists in the post-Stonewall gay community and that desire is always in the process of being socially marginalized in one way or another. Davies's effectiveness as a queer auteur, then, comes out of an expression of his own personal marginalization rather than ideology.

Davies pushes Tucker's complicated desires into the realm of the sadomasochistic, so that the already profound religious guilt he feels over his own homosexuality is exacerbated by the shame he feels as a social aberration who does not even fit in to his ostensible community. Furthermore, the conflation of sex and violence, pleasure and pain, connects Tucker's adult persona irrevocably to that of the pubescent Tucker, whose entire educational experience as presented in *Children* is predicated upon dominant-submissive power games between master and pupil—the sadism enacted on the students by school authority figures is further explored in *The Long Day Closes*, its many scenes of teachers caning their students' hands for minor insubordinations allowing for an even greater continuum of sadomasochistic dynamics across Davies's autobiographical films. Tucker is therefore harnessed to his childhood and its attendant fears, rituals, and eroticisms, even as an adult sexual being. Sex becomes a necessarily shameful act, not simply for the reasons connected to the social stigma of homosexuality and the religious damnation it promises, but also because the act implicitly returns Tucker to a state of pubescence, therefore retroactively making "dirty" the hallowed, virginal ground of childhood.

In *Madonna and Child*, following a scene in which a wheezing, coughing coworker at Tucker's stifling, airless office asks him, out of dull politeness, what he did over the weekend, Davies immediately cuts to Tucker in his bedroom late at night, quietly slipping on a leather jacket and boots. As he creeps downstairs, cloaked in darkness, Davies shows Tucker's mother, lying awake in bed, noticeably aware that her son has surreptitiously left the house despite his best efforts to exit in silence. It is unclear whether this is a literal flashback to what Tucker actually did this past weekend and therefore an image summoned in response to his coworker's question, or if it represents one instance of many like it. Then, in a stunning chiaroscuro composition, we see Tucker in close-up as he knocks on the door of a basement bar; the actor Terry O'Sullivan, with his naturally hollowed cheeks funneling down to two pouty lips that appear as if they're about to slough off his face, never looks more dramatic than in this shot, which bathes him in shadow so deep that we cannot see his eyes. It's clear that he hasn't come to this establishment often, as the bouncer at the door is distrustful of him, questioning him mercilessly and finally slamming the door's grille in his face.

Rejected even by the underground gay community, Tucker embodies a double social shame, and it is implied that he must seek out ever more sordid arenas for sexual thrills, as shown in a scene of a urinal hookup and in highly stylized shots of erotic encounters: these include in *Madonna and Child* an image of Tucker performing oral sex on a man while squeezing his buttocks (which, taking over the entire frame, obscures the act from the camera and de-eroticizes it) and another of him on his knees sucking on the finger of a curly-haired tattooed man like a lollipop. Both of these scenes occur as though in a void, surrounded by enveloping blackness, a space of geographical indeterminacy and atemporality, at once fantasy and nightmare, gratification and guilt. This sort of composition occurs again in *Death and Transfiguration*, when, following a moment in which Tucker tenderly says to his ailing mother, "Oh Mam, what would I do without you?" Davies cuts to an image of an African American man in leather cap and sunglasses telling a submissive man kneeling before him wearing a zipper-mouthed leather hood to "use your fucking teeth." It's unclear whether the slave is Tucker and this is a literal memory from his past, or just a visualization of an erotic fantasy. In Davies's cinematic world, it doesn't matter—dream and reality are hopelessly, tremulously intermingled, and as a socially marginalized figure seeking a personalized queer aesthetic, he is forced to carve out a realm of the unreal, a locale of indeterminate time and space on which he can project his desires.

The most memorable instance in the *Trilogy* expressing Tucker's simultaneous shame and desire is also one of the most daring dissociative aesthetic choices of Davies's career—queer in both literal and figurative senses. In *Madonna and Child*, not long after we see a tense Tucker walking past a tattoo parlor, we hear in voiceover his phone call to a tattooist. The uncomfortable conversation consists of Tucker asking, in a desperate and hushed tone, if he will tattoo his "bollocks," and the artist awkwardly deflecting the request with a series of hedges, until he finally hangs up on him. What's most striking is the visual accompaniment to this odd dialogue: while we hear Tucker basically pleading for the tattooist to bestow on him both pain and pleasure, Davies has situated us in a church. The camera slowly tracks from left to right over the first six Stations of the Cross, indicating that Tucker's sexual frustrations emanate from an inner battle between faith and sexuality. Here, his every utterance feels like the gasp of a tortured soul, a yearning for transcendence through the desecration of flesh, and the distanciation forced on the audience through the juxtaposition of sound and image unleashes a discomfiting, unavoidable queerness on the formal level. It's a scenario that Davies would return to in prose form. In his novel

Hallelujah Now, the protagonist, also Robert Tucker, makes a phone call to the tattooist, and they have the same conversation, though it's more shockingly detailed. It stands out less within the context of *Hallelujah Now*, however, as the book is more besotted with references to its main character's sadomasochistic desires. Its entire second section consists of letters between Robert and various like-minded men, mostly dominants, with whom he has struck up correspondences through personal ads. It is worth noting the explicitness of these passages as a marked contrast to Davies's relatively tame depictions of gay eroticism onscreen, although in both cases sexuality is inferred as a cerebral as much as physical act, thus words are illustrated as being as powerful sexual tools as bodies.[2]

As in *Hallelujah Now*, the main character's crippling guilt over his gayness pushes the autobiographically tinged *Trilogy* irrevocably into the realm of fiction. "In the *Trilogy* I was not only exploring literal truth—my relationship with my mother and father, my religious and sexual guilt—I was also examining my terrors," wrote Davies in *A Modest Pageant* (x–xi). While the timeframe of *Children*, toggling between memories of an unhappy childhood and a tortured young adulthood, matches squarely with Davies's own past (it was made when he was in his early thirties), both *Madonna and Child* and *Death and Transfiguration* create an imagined future, one based on the fears of damnation instilled in Davies as an adolescent that would seem to result from his homosexuality. The middle-aged Tucker doesn't necessarily represent anyone from Davies's reality as much as what he is terrified he could become—or could have become, we can infer, if not for his outlet as a filmmaker and artist. Tucker does not seem to have any creative aspirations. Rather, he has persisted in his life of stifling office drudgery, modeled after Davies's own miserable workaday experiences as a teenager, long left behind; he continues to live with his mother, mixing her cocoa and reading newspaper astrology charts to her in an unbearable intimacy, when he's not sneaking out of the house late at night for trysts; he remains sexually hungry yet chronically dissatisfied, like an adolescent, still fantasizing erotic release rather than achieving it, as expressed in his few visualized sadomasochistic dreams; and he still attends church, even going to confession—this despite Davies's becoming a lapsed Catholic at age twenty-two. Expressing the essential differences between Davies and Tucker, Wendy Everett writes, "Davies himself had to escape the containment of Liverpool before he could, through these very films, find the way to express his own identity. Since Tucker has no such possibility, he is condemned to remain a perpetual misfit" (51).

The most disturbing example of middle-aged Tucker's fear for his own soul comes in a sequence near the conclusion of *Madonna and Child* in which he imagines, in a vividly depicted nightmare, his own death and judgment. First we see Tucker as a pallbearer in a lonely funeral, and then we gradually come to realize that the body inside the coffin is his own. Tucker wakes up screaming; his aged mother, in silhouette at the door, checks in on him. No such comfort comes in *Death and Transfiguration*, which, as the Catholicism-evoking title indicates, concludes the *Trilogy* with both morbidity and catharsis. Though the film liberally skips around in time—from a point in Tucker's childhood even earlier than that in *Children,* to middle-age, to elderliness—and was thus far Davies's most temporally experimental work, *Death and Transfiguration* has an anchoring present, set in a geriatric ward. Since Tucker's childhood seemed to exist in a past recognizable as the late 1950s or early 1960s, one can project that, though no year is given, this last part of the *Trilogy* is largely set in some unspecified future, presumably the dawn of the twenty-first century. The now-infirm Tucker is played by an actor in his early seventies, Wilfrid Brambell, known best to Davies and the general British public from his starring role in the sitcom *Steptoe and Son* (1962–74).[3] The film closes with Tucker's death, which takes place on a lonely Christmas Eve and is represented as an entrance into a void and a moment of spiritual transcendence. His eyes open wide, in an expression that could be read as either terrified or calm, and he reaches out, a white light enveloping the room. The ambiguity of the moment is disturbing—it is clear from the *Trilogy's* entirety that Tucker believes himself to be damned. An a capella rendition of "You're Still the Only Boy in the World," ostensibly sung by the character's mother, wafts over the sound track in his last moments, an ironic commentary on Tucker's isolation, constant and now eternal. In the seconds before his passing, Tucker sees a vision: a silhouette of a bare-chested man in front of the window; in his outline we can see a young, well-developed physique. The figure could be one from his past, or a dark angel. Even in his ultimate breaths, Tucker conflates spirituality and eroticism, expressing both terror and elation, pain and pleasure, when faced with the unknown. Unredeemed by pride and disqualified from achieving a sexual identity deemed socially acceptable, Tucker dies anonymously and alone, a man outside of love and time.

Outside Women

Terence Davies's social, sexual, and artistic outsider status is reflected onscreen even in his adapted works, most prominently in his main female characters, with whom Davies seems to hold an affinity. There is a hint of this distaff identification in *The Neon Bible*, but Gena Rowlands's Aunt Mae, though embodied with a vivaciousness that often puts her front and center in the narrative and the frame, is not the protagonist. Much as *The Neon Bible* has been considered, even by Davies, a transitional work, a test-run of sorts for future adaptations, Davies's casting of Rowlands (whom the director claims to have regarded as perfect for the role upon first reading John Kennedy Toole's book) anticipates his work with major female actresses in lead parts, specifically Gillian Anderson in *The House of Mirth* and Rachel Weisz in *The Deep Blue Sea*. Rowlands's Aunt Mae—a loving and eccentric yet emotionally distant relative to the film's pubescent protagonist—is an intrinsically queer figure, an eternally lonely yet colorful and performative misfit who rejects the normal domestic lifestyle; yet she's also largely cut from the same cloth as the older sisters and wily, self-sufficient friends and neighbors that populate *Distant Voices, Still Lives* and *The Long Day Closes*. Anderson's Lily Bart and Weisz's Hester are more radical female creations for Davies, however. Terence Rattigan's Hester may ultimately save herself from the tragic fate that befalls Edith Wharton's Lily, but they are social outsiders with whom Davies clearly sympathizes. Pariahs though they may become, Lily and Hester are never victims, both firmly in charge of their own destinies, refusing to play by society's rules dictating what they are supposed to be and whom they are supposed to love. Their downfalls are ironically the results of a surfeit of principles, an unwillingness to jeopardize their integrity. The fortitudes of Lily and Hester that characterize the later fictional works of Davies's career could be seen to represent a newfound confidence and strength in the director himself, one related to matters of social and sexual identification.

In 2000, *The House of Mirth* certainly seemed like Davies's least characteristic film. Set between 1905 and 1907 within the drawing rooms, opera-house loges, and glistening yachts of the New York City social elite, it took the director far from working-class Liverpool. It was a more surprising choice for adaptation than his last American excursion, *The Neon Bible*, the subject matter of which at least offered some of Davies's hallmarks—adolescence, abjection, abuse. Even Davies agreed, telling Graham Fuller in *Film Comment*: "It's the first work that's different from everything else I've done. Obviously it doesn't have the same kind of passion you have when you're dealing with things you've actually gone through or that the people that you grew up with and loved went through" ("Summer's End" 55). Yet *The House of Mirth* nevertheless is imbued with remarkable passion, and it comes greatly from Davies's intense focus on Anderson's Lily, who is nearly always onscreen and whose gradual emotional decline Davies films with a studied yet profound compassion one might compare to that of the masterful Japanese director Kenji Mizoguchi, who, in such devastating films as *Sisters of the Gion* (1936), *The Life of Oharu* (1952), and *Street of Shame* (1955), granted his many tragic female protagonists grace amidst suffering at the hands of a cruel society. Davies's film is a similarly excoriating tragedy on a social scale. Never quite fitting into the world of wealth and decorum into which she has been brought by her wealthy aunt, Lily is a bit of a social neophyte, unable to read and interpret the codes of the finely calibrated, viperous environment she tries to navigate. Though she has, as she says, "the reputation for being on the hunt for a husband," she refuses to marry for any reason other than love, a righteousness that ends up compromising her. Whether or not she realizes it, Lily's moral centeredness and unwillingness to play by "the rules of the game" (as accused by Dan Aykroyd's piggish Gus Trenor after Lily will not sleep with him to return his favor of investing money for her) make her something of a modern woman, and thus she is treated with ruthless distrust. "I suppose the thing that warmed me to Lily is that I feel like an outsider," said Davies to Fuller. "Even though I'm the youngest of ten children and loved my mother, especially, and my sisters and brothers very much, I still felt as though I was looking in on something" ("Summer's End" 55).

Wharton's Lily Bart has been recouped by some scholars as a queer figure, a status that makes her all the more useful and emotionally compelling for Davies. Using the term "queer" less in the modern, academic sense as a signifier of outsider status informed by homosexuality, and more in terms of an individual's relationship to society as a whole, whether based on race, gender, or other, Lori Harrison-Kahan identifies a line from late in Wharton's novel in which Sim Rosedale, one of Lily's many prospective (and least wanted) suitors, rejects her as marriage material and explains, "If I married you now I'd queer myself for good and all, and everything I've worked for all these years would be wasted" (270–71). Rosedale, a wealthy Jewish businessman who has gradually assumed a place of status in New York society, thus identifies Lily as a possible negative influence on his reputation. As a Jew, and therefore an outsider figure himself, Rosedale has placed Lily on a low social rung, one that Harrison-Kahan argues is as derivative of her white womanhood (which socially was "in the process of being queered") as by her financial improprieties and the rumors that her former friends have been spreading about her: "In implicating Lily as one who could 'queer' him, Rosedale draws attention to the new status on the margins of society and reveals the instability of her sexual, racial, and class identities" (35). Though Davies considerably softens the depiction of Rosedale—who in the novel is sketched with a latent anti-Semitism on the part of the author yet played with a doughty kindness by Anthony La Paglia in the film—he does include a passage from the novel that speaks to those levels of social anxiety to which Harrison-Kahan refers. Late in the film, following Lily's devastating humiliation at the hands of the sinister Bertha Dorset (Laura Linney), who publicly casts her off of her yacht under false accusation of a dalliance with her husband, Lily agrees to have tea with Rosedale. At one point, he pointedly says to her: "I know the quickest way to queer yourself with the right people is to be seen with the wrong ones." The implication—that Lily is one of the "wrong ones" and that to interact with her, sexually and socially, would be inherently deleterious for him—is clear, as is Davies's alignment with his increasingly marginalized protagonist.

More frightening to the status quo than Lily's outcast status, however, is her confidence in her own romantic principles and dignity. Thanks to an opportunistic hotel maid, she comes into possession of adulterous love letters that will shame her enemy Bertha and at the same time recuperate her public image; however, the object of those letters' affection, Lawrence Selden (Eric Stoltz), is the man she loves—as is clear from the film's opening scenes, when Lily and Lawrence meet by chance at the Grand Central train station and proceed to spend a flirtatious afternoon in his bachelor flat. Of relatively low income and social standing, Lawrence, still trying to make his way in New York society, is deemed inappropriate husband material. Yet the flame Lily holds out for him indicates not only her independent thinking but also her sexual strength, which only further enrages such men as Gus Trenor and Sim Rosedale. Harrison-Kahan equates this with homosexual individualism: "The threat of women's subjectivity is specifically understood as the threat of sexual agency, both female heterosexual and homosocial desire must be suppressed" (44). Yet as an ideological outsider who simultaneously maintains the proper social decorum, Lily is also constantly playing a part; another aspect of her queerness is that she's always inhabiting a role for social purposes. Lily may be perceived as being "on the hunt for a husband," but she's also searching for her own identity, lost as it is in layers of performativity. This is felt acutely in the film in Anderson's highly mannered acting, a mesmerizing compendium of poses, mannerisms, and secretive smiles, examples of what Jim Ellis calls "a self-conscious performance of selfhood" ("Temporality" 175).

In interviews at the time of *The House of Mirth*'s release, the director invoked such films as Max Ophuls's *Letter from an Unknown Woman* (1948), Douglas Sirk's *All That Heaven Allows* (1955), and Henry King's *Love Is a Many-Splendored Thing* (1955) as influences, whether conscious or not. "I suppose it's primarily about a woman, and I grew up on what used to be called 'The Woman's Picture' . . . they influenced me. But *The House of Mirth* is a great tragedy. A great modern tragedy. And Lily herself is a great tragic heroine" (qtd. in Everett 223–24). Classically, such tragic heroines have been a source of identification for gay male directors, as in the works of Rainer Werner Fassbinder and Todd Haynes, who, like Davies, have often recontextualized melodrama within an art-film aesthetic in films like *Ali: Fear Eats the Soul* (1974) and *Far from Heaven* (2002), respectively. As Jim Ellis writes, "By placing Bart in the heritage of the Hollywood melodramatic heroine, the film makes Lily, along with Aunt Mae and Countess Olenska [the female protagonist of Wharton's *The Age of Innocence*], available for the kind of identification with the tragic and glamorous outsider that frequently marks one version of the queer subject" ("Temporality" 176). Lily's queerness, though interpretable in myriad ways related to gender, performance, and social status, remains a clear entry point with which to regard *The House of Mirth* as a personal work from Davies.

It is difficult to imagine Davies making a film that focuses exclusively or intently on a character who could be deemed a social insider. As Jeff Reichert argues at *Reverse Shot* online, "It's his choice of *The Neon Bible* and then *The House of Mirth* for adaptation, outsider tales both, that more clearly signal how his background on the margins of rigid homosexual-unfriendly orthodoxy led to a kinship with loners, dreamers, and those who don't quite fit in." His third adapted film, *The Deep Blue Sea*, fits perhaps most easily into this hypothesis. It has long been rumored, even assumed, that Terence Rattigan's 1953 play was itself a thinly veiled account of homosexual desire, as the suicide of Rattigan's lover Kenneth Morgan, over another man, is what allegedly inspired Rattigan to write it (Rebellato xviii–xix). More pertinently, perhaps, than the gender of the characters is that the plot revolves around unfashionable, socially unacceptable sexual desire. Davies made major changes to Rattigan's text that wed the film more completely and coherently to Hester's point of view. Rattigan's first, greatly expository act—in which Hester's landlady and neighbors discover her body on the floor of her flat following a suicide attempt and proceed to fill the audience in on the main players and their dramatic conflict—is mostly tossed out, in favor of a more subjective and suggestive exploration of its main character's emotional state, resulting in a largely wordless, ten-minute prelude that drifts in and out of disconnected moments from Hester's past with her lover, Freddie Page (Tom Hiddleston), and her husband, the judge William Collyer (Simon Russell Beale), set to Samuel Barber's swooning Violin Concerto. The rest of the film, likewise, frequently jumps from the established present (the day following Hester's near-death) to moments in the past, many of them Davies's inventions.

Hester's decision to leave her caring, tried-and-true husband and the life of comfort and wealth he represented for an unstable, relatively impoverished, yet sexually enticing existence with the much younger, handsomer Freddie is reflective of gay longing and its attendant social stigma and marginalization. It is worth noting, also, that *The Deep Blue Sea* contains what can be termed Davies's only real sex scene. Though there have been instances of explicit homoeroticism in his films, never before had there been glimpses of romantic coupling. During the swooning ten-minute fever dream that opens *The Deep Blue Sea*, we see overhead shots of Hester and Freddie in bed, their naked hands exploring each other's bodies as the camera swirls overhead. In one surprising expression of carnality, Hester licks Freddie's bare shoulder from behind; Davies's momentary fixation on this seemingly spontaneous bit of body contact makes it more than a passing fancy. Hester is *enjoying* the touch, the taste of Freddie smooth, young skin—one can assume a textural change from her husband's—and with this brief yet definitive moment of eroticism Davies establishes that his film will partly concern Hester's pleasure. This sets up Hester as a defiant figure, as female sexuality, especially in England in 1950, would be considered an aberration. In this way—in seeking physical gratification—Hester is defying convention, dodging "the rules of the game," to recall Gus Trenor. Furthermore, the blatant objectification of the male body in this sequence invokes the queer perspective of desire that fuels *The Deep Blue Sea*, redirecting the male gaze and visually repositioning the film away from the realm of standard, classically heterosexual romance.

Davies's aesthetic choice to visually evoke David Lean's *Brief Encounter* (1945) also serves to place *The Deep Blue Sea* in a continuum of British drama in which repressed heterosexual romance functions as a metaphor for gay desire. Based on Noël Coward's short play *Still Life*, about a housewife whose drab domestic routine is upended when she meets and falls in love with a handsome, married doctor at a train station, *Brief Encounter* has been a major influence on many filmmakers in its eloquent, fragile depiction of restrained, seething passion. Coward's story (which he adapted for the screen himself) has been particularly appreciated by gay audiences, with Celia Johnson's portrayal of Laura Jesson viewed as a devastating, concealed essaying of gay repression as much as female social subjugation. In his BFI book on *Brief Encounter*, Richard Dyer writes, "The subject matter—forbidden love in ordinary lives—makes an obvious appeal to gay readers, as do fear of discovery and settling for respectability (Laura's home is her closet)" (11). Davies has revealed that at least two sequences he added to *The Deep Blue Sea* were direct homages to *Brief Encounter*—scenes of William and Hester in the calming yet stifling environment of his study, recalling the images of Laura at home with her husband, and a late-film shot in which Hester nearly throws herself in front of an oncoming train, the camera capturing her desperation in extreme close-up as the wind from the locomotive whips about her hair dramatically and its lights flash on her face. Such grandly tragic gestures are reminders of the film's debt to melodrama, and thus that Davies's queer perspective is a particularly apropos connection to that generic tradition, which is given to such bouts of fatalism. The queer artist's attraction to the outsized emotions of melodrama recalls, according to Heather Love, "the association between homosexual love and loss—a link that, historically, has given queers special insight into love's failures and impossibilities (as well as, of course, wild hopes for its future)" (23). Impossibility and doom are traditional, if outmoded, key words for queer identity in much of the twentieth century, so it would follow that the narratives of much queer art would be fueled by heartbreak.

It is not only in its maker's identification with his queered protagonist, however, that *The Deep Blue Sea* can be marked as further evidence of Davies's ongoing fictional-autobiographical project. As Geoff Andrew wrote in *Sight & Sound* upon the film's U.K. release, "Anyone well acquainted with Davies's work will hardly be surprised by the film's postwar setting, its concern with frustrated desires, dashed hopes, loneliness, and oppressive social constraints, and its formal audacity, invention, and elegance" (18). More than that, Davies bestows upon Hester his family's memories of growing up in working-class Liverpool in the immediate postwar period, retrieving Rattigan's depiction of London in the 1940s and 1950s as fully his own. The emotional damage sustained by Freddie as an RAF pilot in the war, which fuels the violence simmering below his affair with Hester and grants their relationship a palpable instability, is left as back story in both play and film, yet Davies, born right after the war ended and haunted by his family's stories of civilian survival (as memorably dramatized in a jarring flashback in *Distant Voices*), more liberally literalizes the scars of the war that remain present in its characters' lives. One of Davies's greatest flourishes is an interlude in which Hester remembers hiding out with William in the subway tunnels during the Blitz, along with a mass of folks. It is filmed as a single extended shot, which begins on a family huddled on the train tracks and then slowly yet grandly tracks left while the terrified people sing along to the Irish standard "Molly Malone" until the camera finally reaches

Hester and William, standing on the far end of the platform. In explicitly referencing this trauma—a moment when Hester was on the verge of life and death—and pairing it with a familiar folk song that might have been sung in one of the parlors of *Distant Voices, Still Lives* or *The Long Day Closes*, Davies makes an auteurist statement of intent, merging Hester's painful memories with his own, and confirming that the film is his as much as Rattigan's.

Davies's own past becomes as crucial to the rhythms and philosophies of *The Deep Blue Sea* as the particulars of Rattigan's source material, both in his significant alterations and the ways he envisions the world as conceived by the playwright. A more claustrophobic affair, Rattigan's play is set exclusively in the drab Ladbroke Grove townhouse flat where Hester has moved with Freddie. Though Davies has opened the play up, the film is similarly ensconced in the apartment's grim, creaking, wallpapered environment, the type of place that Davies has claimed to know intimately: "I remember those bleak rooms very well. My sister moved into one, and God I hated it. It was that dark twenties furniture and that cheap grey marble. I can just see that room," he said in an online interview with *Little White Lies* (Woodward). One of the scenes that Davies added, meanwhile, is directly taken from his own experience. An extended flashback of Hester and Sir William visiting his icy, condescending mother was based on a weekend Davies spent meeting the mother of a woman he once tried to date ("the most miserable weekend of my life," he has claimed [qtd. in Andrew 22]). Such connections further align Hester with Davies. She doesn't fit—with her husband, with her lover, with the upper or the working class, in a posh estate or in a gloomy rooming house—but, as the final scene intimates, she will live to see another day, even if she doesn't find her place in this world.

In speaking of the impossible choices life has thrown her way, Hester believes herself to be "caught between the devil and the deep blue sea." All of Davies's protagonists—Tucker, Bud, David, Lily, the siblings in *Distant Voices, Still Lives*—are similarly stuck in the queer space between worlds, lost souls who seem to exist out of the time and space of their own lives. Any one of them might have said "I'm an alien in my own land," as Davies does in *Of Time and the City*. The characters often retreat into memory, or their idealized vision of the world. This allows Davies's oeuvre to be both classical and formally radical, a combination

I'll later look at in more depth. In *Hallelujah Now,* Davies describes Robert's middle-age thusly: "He fell into a constant looking back to a past which had never really existed, he fell into a constant dreaming in nostalgia which dulled the edge of failure" (53). Davies's invented pasts and imagined futures create a filmic world that is akin to a haunting.

The Elation of Melancholy

In a 1992 *Sight & Sound* interview about the techniques he and his crew used to evoke the authentic yet dreamlike 1950s Liverpool of his adolescence in *The Long Day Closes,* Terence Davies broke into a recollection of seeing *Singin' in the Rain.* Davies has many times recalled the 1952 Technicolor musical as his first film, as well as one of his favorites.[4] On this occasion, Davies was explaining the effect he was going for in a particular scene. In it, young Bud is waiting outside the cinema, asking adult passersby to escort him into the theater, as a near monsoon of rain cascades down around him. It is clearly movie rain, a heightened effect and, as it turns out, an homage to the first film Davies ever saw. In recalling *Singin' in the Rain,* Davies exalted, "During the big sequence I just cried and cried because I thought this was such happiness, I'll never know such happiness again—it breaks my heart" (qtd. in Kirkham and O'Shaughnessy 15).

 That a memory of happiness should "break his heart" is a key to unlocking the queer emotional state of Davies's films. When writing about his oeuvre, critics tend to use telling contradictions. "He has made some of the most miserable films in the history of cinema, all of them illuminated by glimpses of pure joy" (Hattenstone, "Bigmouth" 5). "The Davies mode is a controlled, perhaps depressed, ecstasy" (Hoberman, "Long Day" 42). "He envisions dark, realistic despair and bright, pop-culture hope as the essence of modern existence" (White 133). "The overall effect is one of muted rapture, a swelling ecstasy held in check by a constant tug of sadness" (Lim 17). These paradoxes speak to a director whose films have represented trauma—abuse, sadomasochism, religious dread, loneliness, suicide, murder—but who wrote, in *A Modest Pageant,* "My earliest influences couldn't have been more jolly, couldn't have been less grim" (ix). As a result of a crucial juxtaposition of subject matter and tone, his films are more often elating, even transcendent, than they are weighted down. That Davies manages to achieve ethereality in much of his work seems miraculous, and speaks to an off-kilter sensibility that contains echoes of that mixture of tragedy and unabashed theatricality often aligned with queer art and performance. In such instances, love and joy are inextricable from their impossibility. In Davies's case, the search for a lost happiness, often associated with childhood, is a gesture toward utopia. According to Jim Ellis, this very discrepancy between a real life and an opposing fantasy one is itself queer: the performed past and the actual past are united in a "collective performance of reality" ("Terence Davies" 141). The aesthetic incongruities of Davies's films reflect the balance of abjection and exaltation within the queer experience. Writes Heather Love, "This contradiction is lived out on the level of individual subjectivity; homosexuality is experienced as a stigmatizing mark as well as a form of romantic exceptionalism" (3).

This "romantic exceptionalism" is what allows Davies to overcome, at least aesthetically, the stigma of homosexuality. These are films that neither wallow in the past nor completely embrace the promise of the future, so their emotional tenor—which Sianne Ngai, in her study of the aesthetics of negative emotions, might call a "non-cathartic state"—is trickily achieved on a filmic level. In the previous section, I examined the deeply personal content of Davies's films, how they are imbued with his past and identity; here we shift focus to how he creates those worlds onscreen through music, cinematography, and editing, and therefore how he visualizes that precarious balance—between triumph and tribulation, wistfulness and torment—that is his cinematic signature and which has resulted in one of the most idiosyncratic careers in narrative film. The simultaneous joy and melancholy that Davies makes viewers feel cannot, of course, merely be willed onto the screen by virtue of the director's outlook or autobiography; the singular effect of his films is the result of specific and meticulous aesthetic choices.

A description of Davies's working methods is first in order. Before he begins production, Davies spends a period of approximately ten to twelve months making extensive notes; these can include fully conceived sequences alongside partial ideas, images, and scraps of dialogue. These notes eventually form something resembling a narrative, from which he constructs the actual screenplay. This first draft is perhaps the most essential to his artistic identity: in it, he maps out the entire film, including camera setups, cuts, dialogue, and musical selections—all is preplanned, and little is ever drastically altered from this blueprint. He has said, "Every track, every pan, every bit of dialogue, everything is in it, and that's what I shoot. I don't improvise at all. I mean, I may add an odd close-up here, or a pick-up shot there, but that's very rare" (Dixon 191). Following this, to get some distance from the material, he puts it down, and then after a period of four to six weeks returns to it and embarks on a second draft. This is the script that is shot, with only minor deviation; the screenplay is so detailed that Davies claims to have never done storyboards. With the exception of the occasional particularly complex scene, his rehearsal time is short (he has said only fifteen to twenty minutes before shots), and he prefers to do no more than five takes for each setup. In *A Modest Pageant*, Davies also claimed that once he has assembled the footage for a film, he doesn't again refer to the shooting script. "The images *must* live, the images must *reveal* the story. The intrinsic detail and order changes, but the big sequences always work the first time, with a little tweaking" (xii).

This method—used in every film of his except *Of Time and the City*, which called for a looser form by its found-footage design—sets him apart from other British directors of his generation, such as Mike Leigh, Peter Greenaway, and Ken Loach, all peerless auteurs given to looser, more outwardly collaborative styles, often encouraging improvisation from their actors. Before shooting begins, Davies has the film choreographed in his head; he then requires the craft and expertise of actors, art directors, costume designers, cinematographers, camera operators, lighting crew, and other technicians to help him realize his vision. In an account of his years as head of production for the British Film Institute in his book *The Eloquence of the Vulgar*, Colin MacCabe, who also served as executive producer on *Distant Voices, Still Lives* and *The Long Day Closes*, writes of witnessing Davies on set: "The film existed in every detail before any cast or crew were engaged. At the same time every suggestion or alteration was listened to with great care and, occasionally, some minor detail would be altered or changed, but it was clear that this was only after the most intense reflection by Terence: the calculation of how altering one tiny element of one short scene was going to affect the whole film" (15).

A major reason Davies has claimed this method of filmmaking to be successful for him is that shooting the script exactly as it has been written and mapped out in detail allows him to work without any suspiciousness or second-guessing from producers. "This process gives me a great degree of control. People know exactly what they're getting, and if they turn around and say, 'You can't do that,' you say 'But, I'm sorry, it's in the script. I told you I was going to do that'" (Dixon 191). Such practical matters dovetail splendidly with artistic ones. By maintaining such control over his productions, which in screenplay form are rather unorthodox, Davies instills confidence in his producers and collaborators, while using large and unwieldy film crews to help him create works of great intimacy. After all, the illusion of the widely shared cinematic notion of auteurism is that a film is a single artist's private world laid bare—despite the large number of people it takes to create that world. Davies's particular aesthetic—an atemporal, emotional form more wedded to the unconscious than surface logic—is worth further consideration because it implicitly expresses the mix of melancholia and exaltation that defines the queer experience, and because it could be said to anticipate the current state of moving images, given so easily to nonlinear forms. The distance created by the warring halves of his aesthetic makes Davies's worlds appear and feel remarkably fragile. As noted in the previous section, Lily Bart's queerness in *The House of Mirth* is partly identified by a conscious performance of the self. One could further say that Davies's films are similarly queered in the way that they constitute a performance of reality. His aesthetic distancing techniques are reminiscent of the queer performance of the self—as outlined by Jim Ellis, this is "a performance that comes to be marked by both a pained self-consciousness and an awareness of a founding gap both within the self and also between the self and the world" ("Temporality" 174). Davies's works are constantly finding new ways to cinematically express this seemingly irreconcilable gap.

Sound and Music

A word that permeates writing on Davies's work is "nostalgia," whether invoked positively or negatively. Many critics have fallen back on the crutch of calling his filmography nostalgic simply because it deals with the past in a way that is at times inescapably affectionate. Yet the absence of nostalgia is just as often remarked upon. Tony Williams writes, "Davies attempts traumatic depictions using characteristic techniques of memory fragmentation and nonlinear representation involving his audience in an unpleasurable realm. By doing this he avoids the nostalgia inherent in any work dealing with the past" (246). So, is Davies's work nostalgic or not? If we look at the etymology of the word itself, it might be deemed a highly applicable term for his cinema. Not an expression of sentimentality, *nostalgia* derives from two compounded Greek words, *nóstos* and *álgos*, translating roughly to *homecoming* and *pain*. Thus nostalgia constitutes a mixture of emotions both pleasurable and not, referring as it does to a place and time to which one can never return despite an all-consuming desire to do so. Davies's features—all of them fully or partially period pieces—attempt to aesthetically evoke this particularly queer feeling, defined by a dramatic type of sentimentality connected to a period of presexuality. By looking to the past with a mix of cold pragmatism (acknowledging its horrors) and warm longing (idealizing its joys), Davies foregrounds his own painful negotiations with the aesthetics of identity.

How can a filmmaker convey pleasure and pain, elation and melancholy, in a single camera flourish, cut, or musical selection? At the outset of his career, it would seem that Davies himself would not have been able to answer that question. He has even retrospectively spoken of the *Trilogy* as being too emotionally one-note: "They're incredibly depressing—there isn't a 'gag' anywhere in them!" (Dixon 194). Its first two parts—*Children* and *Madonna and Child*—are particularly morbid affairs, and whatever visual beauty can be found in them is of the atmospheric, almost noirish variety: the chiaroscuro lighting of Tucker's brooding middle-aged visage, the way the camera roams across a forbidding Catholic church interior, the shadowy darkness from which naked flesh emerges in a handful of sexual encounters. It's not until the opening of *Death and Transfiguration* that Davies offers an aesthetic strategy that will in part come to define his entire cinematic career. As this final chapter opens, there is a gorgeous, stately long shot of Liverpool, as though seen from the heavens. This is shortly followed by a close-up of the front of a hearse, headlights aimed directly at the camera. The morbid vehicle's reflective black surfaces are then captured in a detailed variety of angles—its doors, its wheels—and we also see inside the car, where two hands are clasped together in mourning. The content of the shots might not seem different from that witnessed in the previous two installments, both of which climax with funerals: that of Tucker's father in *Children*, and then Tucker's vivid nightmare of his own interment in *Madonna and Child*. Yet the sound-track accompaniment to these images immediately alters the disposition of what we're seeing. We come to realize it is Tucker's beloved mother who has died, and as we watch her funeral procession begin, we hear the light piano introduction to Doris Day's "It All Depends on You." Instantly, we are in a tonally disparate film world from what we have seen before. The juxtaposition—between the harsh images and the ethereal love song sung in Day's honeyed, breathy tones—creates a complex mixture of emotions that cannot easily be read as simply despairing, or even as demonstrably poignant, as it also creates a strange, intangible beauty. For the first time, Davies has cast a seemingly ironic glance on the intimacy he has established between mother and son in the previous *Trilogy* shorts. The song, originally from the 1955 film *Love Me or Leave Me* (1955), starring Day as a nightclub performer stuck in an abusive relationship with a gangster, played by James Cagney, concerns its singer's unhealthy dependency on the man in her life. As Day sings, "I can be happy, I can be sad / I can be good or I can be bad. / It all depends on you. / I can be lonely out in a crowd / I can be humble, I can be proud. / It all depends on you," we realize the unhealthy romance of which Day speaks could apply to Tucker's dependency on his mother. Now that she is gone, he will be adrift, potentially unable to choose between happy and sad, good and bad, humble and proud. "It All Depends on You" comes to a delicate, melodic close as the casket is sent to the ovens for cremation.

Davies's adoration of Doris Day is also essential to note here—he often mentions her with infectious delight as one of his favorite entertainers, and he can even be seen in a 1992 episode of the British television-arts magazine series the *South Bank Show*, devoted to the release of *The Long Day Closes*, lip-synching to her voice in a highly stylized act that touches the edges of drag performance. The interjection of this Hollywood icon, known for her sunny disposition and cheerful can-do attitude on screen, into Robert Tucker's drab, fatalistic Liverpudlian world has an undeniable queering effect on the film. The song creates a rupture in not only the film but also the whole trilogy, establishing a strong authorial irony heretofore concealed behind a more earnest realism. It's not surprising that *Death and Transfiguration* will go on to be more structurally experimental than the previous two shorts—Davies's musical interjection has freed him to play more openly with form. It is the most musical of the three, in that it skips through time with abandon, and while it seemingly functions primarily on a logic of free-association, it is made of distinct movements and segments set discretely during Tucker's childhood, middle-age, and elderliness. Wendy Everett proposes that one of the keys to understanding Davies's cinema is the idea of it being shaped and constructed as though music: "In any close consideration of how Davies structures and edits his films, the predominant principles can be recognized as musical, rather than reflecting a more traditional narrative logic" (26). Davies's use of music—from religious hymns to standard pop songs to classical symphonies to opera—is therefore essential to understanding how he evokes his specific brand of joyous melancholy.

It is important to note that the deployment of Doris Day's "It All Depends on You" in *Death and Transfiguration* is particularly significant for being a pop song. For all their austerity, *Children* and *Madonna and Child* are not without music, but in those films it is largely of a traditional variety (the Irish folk ballad "Barbara Allen" memorably closes the former, as the camera floats away from young Tucker, leaving him bereft and on the cusp of adulthood). Day's song not only evokes a particular emotion in the viewer but also calls attention to itself as a cultural touchstone for the filmmaker, an echo from his past. It would be hard to overestimate the essentialness of classic, especially American, standard tunes of the early to mid twentieth century—typified by such composers such as Jerome Kern, George Gershwin, Cole Porter, Harold Arlen, Richard Rodgers and Lorenz Hart, Hoagy Carmichael, Sammy Fain, and Irving Berlin—to Davies's filmmaking. Davies nicely summed up his personal connection to these songs, and the cultural cachet he believes them to possess, when he said in an online interview, "It's poetry for the ordinary, and that American Songbook is unequaled throughout the world. The very best of it is as good as Schubert or Mahler, any of the great song cycles" (Hillis).

The importance of popular music in Davies's life and art is most keenly felt in *Distant Voices, Still Lives*. In the absence of traditional plot mechanics or dialogue that serves to push narrative forward, it is largely composed of what in other films would be deemed musical interludes. Communication between characters is similar to the way Davies imparts information to us as viewers: abstracted and mediated. Especially in the first half, Davies jumps back and forth in time so often, from the 1940s to the 1950s, that there is barely any space allowed for entire, dialogue-driven scenes to unfold. Instead, we get snippets of conversations and fragments of confrontations; events, both fondly recalled (a jaunt at the seaside with Eileen and her friends Jingles and Monica) and traumatic (the scenes in which we see father beating Maisie and mother), begin in medias res and are left unresolved. The film's many singing sequences, then, stand out in sharp relief, as Davies often holds the camera longer on these performances, whether sung in the living room or in the pub, than on any other scenes. As a result, narrative time itself seems to stop—these moments exist in their own chronological framework, an odd in-between space in which the characters reveal themselves to us by wearing the protective guise of performance. Ultimately more of the film's running time is devoted to these tunes than to its spoken dialogue. Because of this, the scenes of casual singing take on a great significance, indicating the warmth and familiarity of community and also standing in for the emotions the characters cannot fully express. Songs become the stories of their lives, making *Distant Voices, Still Lives* something like a musical, albeit a radical one. It is perhaps close to Jane Feuer's analysis of the movie musical as akin to folk art in its idealization of community and ritual in her book *The Hollywood Musical*: "The musical, always reflecting back on itself, tries to compensate for its double whammy of alienation by creating humanistic 'folk' relations in the films" (3). In this way, Davies pays tribute to the working class's indomitable, and often exclusively feminine, collectivity; their singing of giddy, good-natured pop music becomes an act of defiance. Songs like "If You Knew Suzie," "My Yiddishe Momma," "Roll Along Kentucky Moon," "Barefoot Days," "S'wonderful," "Buttons and Bows," and especially "I Want to Be Around to Pick Up the Pieces," belted out by Eileen in *Still Lives* in a moment of quivering bravado, shine like beacons in the dark of a violent, shared, ever-present past.

Singing as community in *Distant Voices, Still Lives*.

As songs exist within our memories, they are necessarily moments out of time, reminders of the power of art to construct identities. Said Davies, "Those songs, prior to rock and roll, they gave ordinary people a voice for their feelings. And I didn't realize then that, when people sang those songs, they were singing something that was deep inside them" (qtd. in Everett 206). The characters in *Distant Voices, Still Lives* are poignant reminders of the following passage in "The Dry Salvages" from T. S. Eliot's *Four Quartets*:

> For most of us, there is only the unattended
> Moment, the moment in and out of time,
> The distraction fit, lost in a shaft of sunlight,
> The wild thyme unseen, or the winter lightning
> Or the waterfall, or music heard so deeply
> That it is not heard at all, but you are the music
> While the music lasts.

The people *are* the music in Davies's films, their profoundest unspoken emotions expressed only through melodies and lyrics, while the songs themselves represent for Davies a sense of shared working-class values. Recalls Davies: "That culture was very rich, because you had to make your own entertainment, which was why when you went to the pub you sang, and then when you came back to the house with some beer you sang again, and then you listened to some records, and they were always American pop records" (Dixon 187).

In a flashback to a happier time in Hester and Freddie's relationship in *The Deep Blue Sea*, Davies implies just how tied to issues of class and community music can be. First, at the tail end of an embrace between the two of them on their couch, we hear the introduction to Jo Stafford's 1952 hit "You Belong to Me," but when Davies cuts to the inside of a pub, the recording cuts out, replaced by the sound of the pub's denizens singing the same song in unison, a cappella. As the camera zeroes in on Hester and Freddie, it's clear that she is fumbling with the lyrics, watching Freddie's mouth to keep up with everyone else. It intimates the social distinction of Hester—a bourgeois woman who married into privilege—from Freddie and his friends, all of whom seem to know the song by heart, perhaps from endless hours singing in pubs. But the power of the music overwhelms any anxiety Hester might have about not fitting in, as Stafford's recording dissolves back in on the sound track, and Davies segues to a wildly romantic medium shot of the two lovers dancing together in another part of the bar, isolated in their own space. Davies's personal memory of this song, a chart-topper in the United States and England, is crucial to understanding its deployment here. He first heard "You Belong to Me" at home following church one Sunday on the BBC program *Family Favourites*: "I walked to the front door and looked out, and all the doors and windows were open and everyone was listening to it" (Fuller, "Ruins" 45)—a moment of cultural cohesion. The notion of a song as an emblem of communal solidarity—as well as a buffer against fear and death—is literalized in *Distant Voices'* flashback to World War II, a scene identified in the script as taking place in 1940. In the midst of an air raid, the three siblings, then prepubescent, are separated from their parents in the neighborhood's scramble to get to a shelter. Eileen, Maisie, and Tony arrive safely, but Father, angry that they have been momentarily lost, slaps Eileen across the face with force, both out of fury and fear that they might have been killed in the Germans' blasts. Seconds later he instructs Eileen to sing. As falling bombs echo all around them, she tentatively warbles the upbeat "Roll Out the Barrel," soon after which everyone huddled in the shelter joins in. The moment serves as a reference to Humphrey Jennings's documentary *Listen to Britain*, which also featured the tune, sung in unison by the patrons at a civilian formal dance, and as reminder of the ability of music to bring people together in times of distress. This anticipates Hester's war flashback in *The Deep Blue Sea*, in which the Irish ballad "Molly Malone" unites the terrified inhabitants of a bomb shelter during an air raid, the song providing brief sustenance to a populace perilously close to hopelessness.

As Rick Altman writes in his seminal study *The American Film Musical*, "The musical invites us to forget familiar notions of plot, psychological motivations, and causal relationships; we must learn instead to view the film sideways, as it were—arresting the temporal flow and sensing the constant parallels between the principals' activities" (28). This sense of the musical as an abstracted narrative that forgoes common ideas of cause and effect is formally applicable to the experimental, atemporal, emotion-based work of Davies. Yet unlike in the common movie musical, the songs in Davies's films are integrated into a complex emotional echo chamber (also including dialogue sound bridges between scenes and in some cases snippets from other movies' sound tracks), so that they seem as much emanations from an authorial voice as from the characters onscreen. *The Long Day Closes*, while cut from the same aesthetic cloth as *Distant Voices, Still Lives*, takes a more internal approach to pop music, implicitly elaborating on its effects on the subconscious. There are instances of the film's characters singing in explicitly performative moments, such as the brothers Kevin and John teasing their sister's friend while washing at the sink with "Once in Love with Amy"; the sharp-tongued neighbor Edna serenading her husband, at whom she more regularly snaps, with "I Don't Know Why (I Just Do)" at a casual living-room gathering; and Bud and his sister mincing through a parlor rendition of "A Couple of Swells" (reminiscent of Judy Garland and Margaret O'Brien's cakewalk in *Meet Me in St. Louis* [1944], another musical informed by a complicated nostalgia, which Davies has cited as one of his favorite films). These scenes evoke what Jane Feuer has noted as "a remarkable emphasis on the joys of being an amateur" (13); though Feuer refers to the amateurs' formal performances (as in the let's-put-on-a-show narratives of Judy Garland and Mickey Rooney), the point is that the musical can fundamentally be based upon our identification with nonprofessional singers and dancers, such as the characters in Davies's films. At the same time, most of the songs in *The Long Day Closes* issue omnisciently from the sound track as nondiegetic, and as such it is implied they can either only be heard by Bud, the ostensible creator of the memories we're watching unfold, or the audience, invited into the act of remembering with the filmmaker.

As it centers on a period of short-lived happiness punctuated by nightmares of the past and intimations of a terrible future, marked by sexual and social alienation, *The Long Day Closes* relies on a precarious balance of rapture and foreboding. Davies establishes this negotiation of tonal registers right from the start. After the film's lengthy opening credits have ceased (more on the durational importance of this sequence later in this book), the camera situates us on a dreary, rain-drenched, nighttime cityscape; a close-up of a street sign informs us that this is a re-creation of Kensington Street, where Davies grew up. As the camera cranes down and slowly creeps forward, the lush introduction to Nat King Cole's 1957 version of "Stardust" swims across the sound track. The song signals that we are about to go down a somewhat literal memory lane. The lyrics are melancholy, but the music is elating; Cole's silky croon and the gentle rise and fall of the orchestration evoke an instant retreat into the past. We only hear the song through its verse, however, so that the last featured lyrics are, appropriately, "Love is now the stardust of yesterday, the music of the years gone by." The song is cut short as the camera tracks in to a rainy tenement's dark, abandoned front staircase. A dissolve transports us back to the same space in an earlier era, now intact and occupied; we officially have entered the realm of memory and the world of the film, all triggered by the echo of a pop song.

Throughout *The Long Day Closes*, music will be linked with Bud's growing consciousness at the same time that it represents Davies's retrospective take on his childhood. There is a simultaneous authorial sophistication and childish naiveté readable in most scenes. For instance, in one lovely sequence, Bud watches as John and his girlfriend Jean bid each other goodnight at the front door. From the child's point of view, their embrace and kiss take on exaggerated romantic tones: they are silhouetted behind the decorated glass door, appearing as though delicate, engraved cameos. On the sound track Davies overlays Judy Garland's gossamer "Over the Banister," a song that hearkens from a particularly atmospheric and evocative scene in *Meet Me in St. Louis*, when Garland's Esther and her boy-next-door John tentatively flirt as he helps her extinguish the lights throughout her house after a party. Here, Bud's pop-culture-besotted consciousness meets Davies's critical reappropriation of that consciousness, creating something like a musical epiphany—reality has become fantasy; Bud's world (and by extension Davies's past) has retrospectively dissolved into illusion.

Davies makes what is maybe his most bravura expression of the power of pop music near the end of *The Long Day Closes*. Bud, solitary as always, stands outside his house after watching his siblings ride away on their bicycles. After he reaches out to grab the iron railing over the staircase that descends from the street to the basement, Davies dissolves to a direct overhead shot of the boy as he proceeds to playfully swing back and forth. The mellifluous strains of Debbie Reynolds's hit "Tammy" (the theme song to the actress's 1957 comic vehicle *Tammy and the Bachelor*) glide over the sound track as the camera begins to track left smoothly and deliberately. From this heightened image of the street, Davies embarks on a series of dissolves to interiors, all of them shot from the same high overhead angle, and all tracking right to left. First, we see the cinema, its smoke-filled projector beam casting a mysterious, rich light over a house packed with patrons; then a church during Mass, a space to Bud no more spiritual than the previous; and then Bud's austere classroom, in which the children rise from their seats and move in formation out of the room. The theater seats, the church pew, and the school desks are all arranged in similar formation, pointed either right or left towards a being—whether movie, deity, or teacher—from which its followers hope to reach some form of knowledge or transcendence. These are the three holy spaces of childhood outside of the home for Bud, and for Davies. That he has chosen to accompany this thematically rich, clearly summative sequence with "Tammy," a saccharine song with superficial, often silly pop-poetic lyrics ("The old hooty-owl hooty-hoos to the dove, / 'Tammy, Tammy, Tammy's in love!'"), rather than a classical or operatic work that would more definitively unite these spaces in splendor, speaks both to Davies's recognition of

Holy spaces of childhood in *The Long Day Closes*.

Bathed in the Fading Light | 73

popular music's importance in creating identity and the reliance of his art on aesthetic juxtaposition. "The audacity of matching seriousness to kitsch is breathtaking," wrote Armond White of this sequence (342). This passage ends where it begins, as Davies dissolves back to an overhead shot of the basement stairs, though this time it's from the opposite side, with the camera peering down from the house's front window, and Bud is not in the frame. The song has ended. Rather than the camera looking down at Bud, the shot is revealed to be from Bud's point of view, as a cut shows him perched at the window, like so many times before. In a graceful, almost imperceptible reversal, we have moved from Davies's perspective back to Bud's. The difference is crucial: Davies is witnessing a world long gone, but Bud is watching the world go by.

With American pop songs so integral to the sensibility and form of Davies's Liverpool films, it is no surprise that when he made his first film set in the United States, this country's indigenous music would play a central role. The character of Aunt Mae, an aging, self-mythologizing performer who has sung at nightclubs across the eastern states, is *The Neon Bible*'s most literal connection to the standard songs of the 1930s and 1940s, when the film is set. Early in the film, after Mae displays for young David her personal scrapbook, containing remnants of her days on stage, Davies takes Mae, and us, into an idealized, shadowy past. Alone on the porch, her memories triggered, she begins lip-synching to her own voice, drifting across the sound track in a tinny echo, as she warbles the 1927 Gershwin tune "How Long Has This Been Going On"; the camera glides around her slowly and tracks left, a move that indicates, as it does so often in the visual grammar of Davies's films, a travel back in time. After a dissolve, we are now in Mae's past, or her version of it. Dressed in a glamorous outfit and vamping before a microphone, she is surrounded by a pitch-blackness that makes her pop from the screen, heightening the unreality of the moment and indicating that we may not be seeing an authentic representation of an earlier time but rather a romanticized version of it. (The amorous, excited lyrics provide a contrast to Davies's melancholy presentation: "Hey, kiss me twice, then once more. / That makes thrice, let's go for four! / What a break, for Heaven's sake, / how long has this been going on?") Rowlands's performance is slightly off-key, but poignantly so, suggesting that Mae's career perhaps never had a chance to blossom beyond the odd dive or roadhouse gig. In this moment, the film has made its most distinct break from its young protagonist's point of view, allowing a perspectival detour that grants Aunt Mae a momentary narrative supremacy. In this scene, and in her later live performance of Rodgers and Hart's "My Romance" at a war benefit, Mae becomes the film's link to a shared musical past; these American standards are tied directly to her personal aspirations and failures.

Mae's acts provide a marked contrast to the pub and living-room sing-alongs in *Distant Voices, Still Lives, The Long Day Closes,* and *The Deep Blue Sea*, which emphasize the camaraderie fostered by pop songs. For Davies, music is an evocation of loneliness as much as a representation of community. Perhaps none of his films are as solitary as *Of Time and the City*, in which the only protagonist is Davies's humble voice, calling out of a timeless darkness. Though essentially a mournful meditation on a lost past, this documentary is imbued throughout with a splendid lightness and remarkable beauty. As discussed earlier, the film contains one of Davies's most pronounced ironic uses of music—an extended sequence of tenement squalor and destruction to the lilting strains of Peggy Lee's rendition of "The Folks Who Live on the Hill." The film is full of more such instances of odd, incongruous beauty. Much of this, however, comes in the form of traditional classical selections: Franz Liszt's piano solo "Consolation no. 3 in D-Flat Major" delicately lulling us during the film's hypnotic prologue; the aching strings of John Taverner's "The Protecting Veil" over images of workers coming to and fro on Liverpool Bay's River Mersey; Popescu Branesti's "Watch and Pray," featuring the soprano Angela Gheorghiu's heavenly vocals, accompanying scenes of domestic working-class life; the swelling second movement to Salvador Bacarisse's Concertino for Guitar and Orchestra in A Minor op. 72 lending grandeur to drab color footage of graffiti-marked, impersonal slums; the triumphal first movement of Gustav Mahler's Symphony no. 2 in C Minor—Resurrection restoring nobility to Liverpool amid images of poverty and, to quote Davies, "a cityscape that is anything but elysian."

Of Time and the City's overabundance of selections from the nineteenth century and earlier speaks to Davies's adoration of classical music, which he has said is his truest love. This is perhaps most evident in the virtuoso, largely wordless opening sequence of *The Deep Blue Sea*, which employs a full nine unbroken minutes of Samuel Barber's passionate Violin Concerto, op. 14, to accompany images of the memories cascading through Hester's mind during her suicide attempt. Armed with an intense passion for and an encyclopedic knowledge of classical music, Davies has made it clear that the form, tone, rhythm, and movement of such music have been his major influence: "My great templates are the symphonies of Bruckner and Sibelius. So they were always in the back of my mind somewhere as a model of how you begin and how you develop as a symphonic artist. And I do think that film is closest of all to music. Notes and chords on their own don't mean anything. They only mean something when you juxtapose them with something else" (qtd. in Everett 204). This theory of music as a series of juxtapositions aligns with Davies's use of music as something like a foreign agent, an element that serves not necessarily to complement but to counter and queer another element. This reveals the essential aesthetic contradiction of music in Davies's work as well as suggesting that those contradictions are essentially classical in nature.

Color and Light

If Davies strikes a note of rapture while excavating a painful past through his employment of music, then he accomplishes this in his mise-en-scène as well. The unique elegance of a Terence Davies film is the result of a remarkably coherent aesthetic: the way his camera, whether static or moving, captures light and color contributes to a peculiar emotional register that reads as both intoxicating and wearied. A significant key to understanding Davies's visual approach is in the process by which he came to *Distant Voices, Still Lives'* singular look. *Distant Voices* was his first color film, following the *Trilogy*, whose unsparing black-and-white often made it feel like an X-ray as much as a motion picture. Rather than luxuriate in his newfound palette, Davies and his crew devised a number of methods that would help the director to take advantage of color's expressiveness yet also place *Distant Voices* in a visual continuum with the earlier shorts. One approach taken by the cinematographer William Diver was using a coral filter to give the image a slightly faded orange tint. Also, during production Davies and his art directors made sure that no primary colors were in front of the camera, other than the women's red lipstick and nail polish. (Hence the most vibrant image is an object of fetish and an abstracted source of identification from Davies's childhood: as a budding gay prepubescent, Davies was fascinated by his older sisters' makeup and was often tasked with buying it for them at the store. As he told me in interview: "Fridays were fabulous, because all my sisters' girlfriends came, and I was allowed to buy their makeup. It was just fabulous." Such a transaction is delightfully dramatized in *The Long Day Closes*.)

According to Davies, this aesthetic decision is an attempt to resurrect the sense of color as lodged in his memories: "In the '50s everything was shabby. The only primary colors we saw were the red, yellow, and blue gummed labels we used to cut out and make figures from in school! So when we went to a Technicolor film, it was overwhelming because everything else felt black and white, even if it wasn't" (Andrew 20). This allows the female characters to stand out like red smears on a gray canvas, symbolizing the warmth Davies feels toward them. Even in a scene as casual as the one in which Eileen and Monica hang about the family house's stoop following a local dance, smoking and trading pleasantries, the women appear indomitable, their scarlet makeup taking on the effect of armor, even if subliminally to the viewer. And in a postproduction decision unusual for the time, the film stock was put through a bleach-bypass process, which desaturates the color in the final wash of the printing. Davies considers this a "hand-tinted" color style—the resulting image has the faded quality of old photographs, while at the same time allowing the odd color to pop.

The idea of the single element, whether light or color, drawing the viewer's eye within a composition or tableau came to even greater realization in *The Long Day Closes*. Said the production designer Christopher Hobbs about that film, "It's like having everything in a room plain and then you have one wonderful splash of color, a bit of carpet or curtain. It makes you think that the whole room is rich when in fact it's not" (qtd. in Kirkham and O'Shaughnessy 13). That sense of richness is difficult to parse, as it's an emotional rather than luxuriant richness, conveyed with the subtlest of brushstrokes. Davies's remarkable visual recall for the 1950s and his insistence on note-perfect detail posed a challenge for his crew. Hobbs said upon the film's release, "There were photographs of nearly every Liverpool street except Terence's and he had no family photographs"; therefore, *The Long Day Closes* "wasn't a re-creation of '50s Liverpool, it was a re-creation of Terence's memory. I therefore went for memory realism" (qtd. in Kirkham and O'Shaughnessy 13). Such a fragile, subjective concept was achieved through set design, costume, lighting, lenses, and camera movement. One way to make this possible was having the audience see through Bud's perspective, creating a child's-eye view of the exteriors. Since the film's Kensington Street was all invented on a set, Hobbs had control over every detail, which included subtly altering shop signs so they were not quite level and twisting and curling railings more than they would have been. The director of photography Michael Coulter's charge from Davies on *The Long Day Closes* was as classical as it was personal. In preproduction, the director offered Coulter two sources of inspiration for the look of the film: books of paintings by such old masters as Vermeer and Rembrandt, and 1950s photographs of Lancashire taken in Kodachrome, which has a distinct high-contrast, rich color palette, minus any garishness. These twin inspirations reflect the gap between how the director remembers seeing the world and how he knowingly romanticizes it through cinema, granting the past a sort of artistic ennoblement. "My favorite painter is Vermeer," Davies has said. "Because I love light falling on a subject, and that light diffusing, I just think it's ravishing to look at" (qtd. in Everett 212). Vermeer's paintings were idealizations of the artist's seventeenth-century Dutch environment, evocations of everyday, often middle- and working-class people that realistically used natural light to create a heavenly plane on Earth. The subjects in Vermeer's paintings are often positioned near a window, frequently just off the left side of the frame, which then casts an intense central light over them, leaving all else to fall abruptly into shadow. Dramatic examples of this include *Woman Holding a Balance* (1664–65) and *The Astronomer* (1668), both of which offer the types of burnished, slightly obscured compositions one often sees in Davies's work. *The Long Day Closes*, with its many images of young Bud staring out the window, is perhaps Davies's most painterly film, never more so than in a meditative sequence that focuses intently on the boy's profile as it is caressed by the reflections of Guy Fawkes bonfire flames on the street. Bud cuts a glowing, solitary figure against the rest of the room, black with shadows, as the robust sound of the British contralto Kathleen Ferrier singing "Blow the Wind Southerly" drifts over the sound track, the traditional English folk song bestowing upon this child's visage a strange augustness. Davies not only imbues his alter ego with an artistic stateliness, he also gifts the hallowed mother figure a notable resplendency. While she scrubs laundry and sings in hushed tones the early twentieth-century standard "If You Were the Only

Images from the working class in Vermeer's *The Milkmaid* and *The Long Day Closes*.

Boy in the World," Davies frames and lights her in a fashion remarkably similar to Vermeer's world-renowned 1657 masterpiece *The Milkmaid,* in which an earthy, sensual worker woman, in rolled-up sleeves, goes about her household chores with a mysterious mix of melancholy and content, half of her face in shadow. Visually connected to a rich European artistic tradition, the mother assumes grandness even in her mundane tasks. Davies has not simply, or even knowingly, evoked classical art; he has given his character and his film a visual nobility drawn from an iconic image of working-class labor.

Classical Dutch painting is also evoked in *The Deep Blue Sea*, a film whose look is otherwise indebted to Davies's memories of English home furnishings of the 1950s, which he recalls as hopelessly drab yet comfortingly so. According to Jonathan Romney in his *Sight & Sound* review, "Visually the film evokes both emotional grandeur and material shabbiness" (58), a synthesis achieved, as in *The Long Day Closes*, through a remarkable attention to detail and a stylistic heightening of those details. Hester's boarding room, for instance, has a potently dilapidated look, thanks to the generally spare furniture and intensely emotional, deep-red wallpaper, which seems to bear down on her. Yet Davies and the cinematographer Florian Hoffmeister manage to fashion visual poetry from such threadbare surroundings. The director told Hoffmeister that in those flats people had only one lightbulb, but that despite the darkness it looked beautiful. Much of the film's beauty seems centered on Hester herself, who becomes the subject of an exquisite cinematic light show. "I always thought that the light should come from inside her," wrote Hoffmeister in *Sight & Sound* (23), and indeed the actress Rachel Weisz seems to perpetually glow, whether illuminated by a single lamp or in the final sequence—in which she throws open the curtains in an act of emotional defiance after her lover has left her for good—a blaze of sunlight. Weisz's aquiline beauty is particularly highlighted in a shot in which, positioned in left-side profile, she gazes out the window smoking a cigarette; Freddie enters and switches on a red and yellow lamp behind her, emitting the room's single source of light other than the afternoon sun streaming in. Unable to tell Freddie of her near-suicide that morning, Hester keeps her back to him, the sun brightening her face and the front of her bathrobe, but the rest of her in shadow.

The influence of painting is also evident in Davies's America-set films. The critic Edward Guthmann likened *The Neon Bible*'s aesthetic to that of early twentieth-century American artists: "When Tierney, Scarwid, and Rowlands walk through town to a nighttime revival meeting, and the camera elegantly follows the movement of the townsfolk toward the tent, it feels like we're watching an Edward Hopper or Thomas Hart Benton painting come to life." Indeed, in this sequence especially, one can ascertain Hopper's clean lines and mysterious light sources as well as the constant furious motion of the regionalist Benton's midwestern-set murals, with their teeming scenes of American life, though no evidence suggests that this was intentional. And in the film's most blatantly painterly shot, Davies holds on David's mother for a remarkable amount of time as she fragilely coos the Irish lullaby "Too-ra-loo-ra-loo-ra" while positioned at the house's front screen door, bathed in an overwhelming illumination that registers as both celestial and damned. This performance, captured in a static image that is watched at a distance by David and Aunt Mae, is meant to represent the mother's losing her last grip on reality. It is a break from the reality of the film as well, entering into a personal, even metaphorical realm that has little correlation in John Kennedy Toole's story. The scene is notable for the way it instantly connects the character of David's mother to Davies's continuum of benevolent, weary maternal figures simply through the uses of a plaintive song and dramatic, painterly lighting.

For *The House of Mirth*, Davies has been particularly vocal about his visual influences. In a 2000 interview with Simon Hattenstone for *The Guardian*, he told the story of the casting of Gillian Anderson, with whose career he had not been familiar: "I was looking for faces that looked like the Singer Sargent portraits of the belle époque, and I said, 'That is a John Singer Sargent face, who is she?'" ("First Steps" 2). That Anderson, who was well-known throughout the American entertainment industry for her Emmy-winning work on the television series *The X-Files*, was originally sought by Davies not for her considerable acting talent but for a certain ineffable quality in her face that reminded the director of late nineteenth-century portraiture speaks powerfully to his approach. Davies certainly was able to harness what he saw in Anderson for the film, as the way she is lit and positioned in the frame is consistently evocative of Sargent's work. A contemporary of Edith Wharton, Sargent was an Edwardian-era American painter renowned in Europe and his homeland for his facility with grand portraiture as well as his later, more impressionist-leaning landscape work, both of which proved him a master of color and light. His most popular canvases remain the many portraits that were commissioned throughout the late nineteenth and early twentieth centuries from members of high society in Boston and New York City. In these, Sargent did not merely fashion realistic likenesses of his benefactors; he created pointed, sometimes enigmatic, images of the cosmopolitan upper classes at a social turning point. That

Sargent was an expatriate who, like Davies, lived much of his life as a celibate, and is now commonly believed to have been gay (some of his most intensely erotic work focuses on wrestling male nudes, which were not displayed in his lifetime), gives his art a crucial air of outsideness. While one would have to stretch to call his portraits direct critiques of high society, there is an ambivalence to them that has been noted, especially fascinating in terms of the burgeoning social and gender-related progressiveness of the period. In *John Singer Sargent: The Sensualist*, Trevor Fairbrother proposes, "It is fair to say that [Sargent's] complicated approach to truth and realism in portraiture reflects the innovations and dilemmas that shaped his era" (93). Davies's evocation of Sargent's work is especially resonant for the manner in which the painter was able to subtly capture the social realities of the period in his subjects' faces, which only on the surface appear to betray nothing. There is also a sensuality about his portraits that seemingly stands at odds with the propriety they ostensibly depict. All these ambiguities are present in Gillian Anderson's performance, appropriate considering that Lily Bart is a confounding combination of naiveté and grace, a seemingly savvy member of moneyed society who is nevertheless ultimately a desperate outsider. Anderson's every smile is at once guarded and guileless, every tiny gesture (the way she delicately holds a cigarette, slices apart the pages of a book with a letter opener, or barely fingers the ivory keys on a piano in an empty room) both mechanized and charmingly authentic. Is she a victim of the hermetic, fashionable world around her, or is she in control of her own destiny? Such contradictions align Lily with Sargent's portraits, the subjects of which often seem lost behind swathes of their own finery. Sargent's famous lounging *Lady Agnew of Locknaw* (1892), for example, clothed in a sheer, cream-colored dress and lavender sash, is reminiscent of Anderson's enigmatic embodiment of Lily Bart. Lady Agnew stares directly back at us with an expression both lazily content and anticipatory, as if she's considering her next move. One arm is draped behind the left side of her chair in what seems like a casual pose, but the grip of her hand on the side of the chair betrays the intensity in her position. Carter Ratcliff wrote, "Lady Agnew's face seems all possibility, and consciously so. The moment of the right side of her lips look slightly drawn back, as if in doubt or weariness, the left side seems almost to smile. And, as if to insist on her control of this ambivalence, her eyes are oddly calm" (161).

These words could be describing Anderson's face throughout the first half of *The House of Mirth,* before Lily is cast out of society. Whether fending off the advances of the boorish and married Gus Trenor, flirting with unwanted potential suitors like Percy Gryce and Sim Rosedale, or engaging in emotionally loaded banter with the man she truly loves, Lawrence Selden, Lily's face is often locked in a half-smile, evidence of a woman trying to play by society's rules but intelligent enough to know that it is all indeed a game, and a repellent one at that.

Sargent's paintings inspire in *The House of Mirth* not only Lily's mysterious nature but also Davies and the cinematographer Remi Adefarasin's general strategy for composition, lighting, and color. An image of Lily strolling through tall grasses next to the seashore in a white dress and matching parasol seems a direct homage to Sargent's 1888 oil painting *Morning Walk.* And there is an earlier, remarkable composition worth closer analysis for its painterly qualities. While waiting in her parlor for Selden to arrive, Lily perches on the far left of a purple couch festooned with differently colored throw pillows and sheets, one hand placed on a book laying on the small table to her right, the other resting in her lap, her gaze directed eloquently downward, her head slightly cocked to the right. She has eased into an image that is a near still life; Davies's filming of the shot is akin to his painting it. The composition—an act of cinematic self-consciousness on Davies's part—is both beautiful and claustrophobic. Said Davies of the film in 2000, "It had to look like John Singer Sargent portraits but also the belle époque, which was crammed with stuff, dark, like a mausoleum. It'd stifle the life out of anybody" (qtd. in Horne 17). Frozen in time and space, Lily appears trapped by the exquisite furniture and clothes of her privileged world. Her positioning in the frame recalls that of the subject in Sargent's remarkable 1911 painting *Repose (Nonchaloire),* in which a woman swaddled in a white dress that effectively doubles as a funeral shroud sits nearly supine on the left side of a couch, her hands clasped. The woman's expression could be read as contentment, although the image clearly is meant to evoke death as much as peaceful slumber. With only the sound of a ticking clock penetrating the silence of her room, the similar image of Lily could be seen as its own presaging of death, the funereal atmosphere of her room anticipating her final moments in her boarding house, which are also bathed in unforgiving afternoon light.

John Singer Sargent's *Repose* and Gillian Anderson in *The House of Mirth*, studies in restless composure.

For *The House of Mirth* to so dramatically mimic an aesthetic tradition outside of the cinematic medium places the film in a nearly uncanny realm and further establishes the distancing aesthetic strategy that defines its queerness. Graham Fuller wrote in *Film Comment*, "There is always, in Davies's cinema, the sense that someone is creating the image and/or watching it" ("Summer's End" 55–56). This elegantly describes Davies's queer self-conscious style, especially in *The House of Mirth*. Just as Lily is ensconced within a suffocating social environment, Anderson is framed within stifling tableaux. This is never more apparent than in a scene in which she appears in front of an admiring audience at a society gathering, fashioned in a tableau vivant inspired, it is announced, by the French Baroque painter Antoine Watteau's *Summer* (1717–18). Baring her shoulders and feet, wielding a scythe, crowned with a wreath of flowers, and flanked by stalks of golden wheat, Lily is an extraordinary vision, a vague hint of a smile on her face betraying her own pleasure at being looked at, perhaps especially by Selden, who is in attendance. There is a striking change from Wharton's text—in the novel this event occurs, yet Lily appears not as a part of Watteau's tableau but rather as a subject in the society portrait *Mrs. Lloyd* (1775–76) by the eighteenth-century painter Joshua Reynolds (141), whose vivid, realistic work one might more closely align with that of John Singer Sargent. In his perceptive analysis of this scene, Fuller interprets this alteration to have heavily metaphorical significance, writing that the Watteau painting evokes Lily's purity and self-consciousness, as well as foreboding her fate to die a virgin: "She is a naïve woman who has bought into the myth of her own feminine beauty, which, by the end of the film, has palpably passed its sell-by date. 'Summer' is over . . ." ("Summer's End" 59). This is true, but there's also something hauntingly remote about Lily's positioning in the Watteau tableau. This sequence represents the visual literalization of Lily's queer social status, as outlined in the prior section of this book; she is never more an outcast figure operating from the inside than at this moment, when she is eroticized and made remote at once. Of this sequence, Jim Ellis writes, "[W]e might also think about how Davies is insisting on the distance between the allegorical figure and the body of the person impersonating it, which is congruent with his approach to the past in general" ("Temporality" 170). Depicted in the tableau as a mythical figure outside of time, rather than the social insider that the Reynolds painting might have suggested, Lily is untouchable to her audience, made ethereal by her own virtue—defined by her refusal to compromise herself to the morally dubious people who conspire against her. Here, the narrative function of painting connotes a disturbing reversal of the essential purpose of art—this is not freedom of expression as much as social entrapment.

Chronicle of a Carpet

To discuss the painterly aspects of Davies's films, however, is not to simply invoke his influences. Davies crafts images that are beholden only to his own artistic sensibility and are unique in narrative cinema for their compositional daring. "I've no idea where my style comes from. I've not studied painting, I've not studied sculpture, it's all just visual intuition" (qtd. in Dixon 190). One of the most talked-about shots in all of Davies's films is a galvanizing image about two-thirds of the way into *The Long Day Closes*. In Davies's published script, it is inconspicuous: the simple sentence "Hold on floor" in no way augurs the impact of the scene as it appears onscreen. As eagerly remarked upon by detractors as well as fanatics, this image is used as an example of both the impressionistic lengths to which he will go and the limits the narrative cinematic form can handle. It was even a primal moment for Gillian Anderson's relationship with Davies—before she was courted to star in *The House of Mirth*, she claimed to have been emotionally stricken by it in *The Long Day Closes*: "I remember sitting in the theater and bursting into tears. There was just something about it that was so rich and so full and said so much, even though it was centered on a rug. I was just blown away by it" (qtd. in Pendreigh). The responses of many audience members were quite different, according to Davies on the audio commentary track for the BFI DVD edition of the film, who says that the shot "caused a lot of controversy. I cannot tell you how apoplectic with anger some people get!" Since it is an immaculate synthesis of all the concerns I have raised as quintessentially Daviesian (music, lighting, color, composition, perspective) as well as an example of the implicitly and unusually confrontational nature of his art, I will dwell upon this image for the remainder of this section—appropriate, since Davies's camera dwells upon it for an inordinate amount of time.

    The sequence directly follows Bud's terrible nightmare of two male hands reaching out to grab him from the shadows of his dark bedroom. Held in his mother's comforting arms after she has rushed to console him, David glances down to the floor, and the camera tracks his gaze, settling on a rug patterned with crosshatched green leaves. The moonlight shining through the rain-spattered window casts cascading shadows on it, giving its expressive design the feel of a living nighttime jungle. Yet Davies doesn't allow the viewer much time to contemplate this pattern, as the screen dissolves to a different carpet, this one knit with irregular shapes, including elongated diamonds, squiggly lines, color patches, and circles; the camera is positioned in such a way that all of these configurations drape vertically down the frame. At first the carpet is covered by what appears to be afternoon shadow, which gives it a colorless uniformity, but then very gradually sunlight begins to dance over its textures, revealing its beiges, whites, grays, and dull oranges.

The sun moves back and forth on the rug as though a glissando across a piano. The camera remains fixed while this play of light occurs, its static positioning made all the more acute by the natural movement of the sunlight. After one full minute of stillness—a cinematic eternity—while the sun seems to peek in and out of clouds, casting alternating patches of shadow and light, the camera unexpectedly begins to slowly pivot to the right, while remaining fixed on the same spot, until finally it tilts up and we see Bud from the back, kneeling on the couch and staring out the window in his usual spot, the curtain draped over him like a veil, the light from outside giving him the sense of glowing from within.

Davies has said that this sequence was, like so many others, based on his memories. In this case, he recalls the occasional boredom of childhood, when he would find himself at home, fixating on small details, such as a rug's pattern. What is particularly fascinating about what the camera reveals when it finally tilts up is that we are not seeing this rug directly through the eyes of Bud, whose gaze is instead directed outside. Since Davies's authorial perspective is so utterly connected to Bud's point of view, we can assume that he, too, is already glancing elsewhere. Rather, the gaze here appears intended to be the viewer's alone, dissociated momentarily from Bud and from the narrative. Davies seems to want *us* to see the world anew; to defamilarize the familiar; to find the loveliness in the odd patterns of a shabby, tattered carpet; to appreciate the beauty of a natural dance of sunlight; to experience boredom, to crave movement, to both fear and embrace stasis; to just look, and to be.

By drawing our eyes to the pattern on the rug so completely, disallowing us from looking anywhere else in the room for an extended period of time, Davies pointedly frames this unremarkable carpet as a self-contained work of art in its own right. Indeed, the pattern, which offers no symmetry or coherent structure (its lines and waves are unsettlingly inconsistent), might strike some as a painterly piece of lyrical abstraction, its coldness put into relief by the sunlight cast upon it. We are forced to consider its shapes as though we have been drawn to them in a museum. The rug acts as a passive, found art object and an active signal to Davies's memories; either way, it is spectacular in its inescapable mundaneness.

Inseparable from the visual splendor of the image is the accompanying music on the sound track. While filming this scene, Davies played on set the piece that would be used in the final cut, so that he could appropriately time every camera rest and movement. The rhapsodic orchestral passage Davies takes from the British composer George Butterworth's "A Shropshire Lad" (1911–12) is splendidly bucolic, instantly adding a naturalism and gravitas to a challenging and modernist cinematic move. Through the music, the scene becomes an unexpected idyll. When the camera is immobile, fixed on the carpet as the light comes in, the music is transporting—a glistening harp conjures images of sun-dappled fields and waving grasses. As the camera begins to rotate, however, violins grow more insistent, and the piece takes on a boldly dramatic, even romantic turn. Timed in this fashion, the music quite blatantly calls attention to the attendant camerawork, almost as though it is instructing the audience to pay attention to the slightest alteration in the image, as perhaps therein lie the secrets to understanding what Davies is doing.

In this way, the scene reveals the inherent self-referentiality of Davies's films. Rather than adhere to the strict naturalism endemic to most memory or autobiographical films, Davies makes the audience aware of the cinematic apparatus that creates these necessarily artificial images. This is indicative of the hyperrealism Davies claims he sought to achieve in *The Long Day Closes*. In *Film Comment*, Graham Fuller called him "the acknowledged master of tableau that, framed and arranged with adroit self-consciousness, memorializes a fragment in time as it passes, or as it is perceived" ("Summer's End" 55). There's no doubt that the rug is a deliberate provocation. In a way, the film's insistent focus on this object is a queering agent, not only for how it implies an identification with a marginalized child on the verge of homosexual puberty but also for the way it forces a close reading—a luxurious lavishing of attention—on an object that another film might consider visual debris. As Elizabeth Freeman writes in *Time Binds: Queer Temporalities, Queer Histories*, "To pause on a given image, to repeat an image over and over, or to double an existing film in a remake or reshoot become productively queer ways to 'desocialize' that gaze and intervene on the historical condition of seeing itself" (xviii). The amount of time that is expended upon our watching and scrutinizing the rug challenges our presumptions about mainstream film grammar. As I'll examine later in this book, Davies's aesthetic is bound up in a queer temporality—which in the carpet's case manifests as a stillness that threatens to place this film outside of traditional notions of time. It is an image that, however unadorned, intends to alter the viewer's perceptions, upending expectations of what cinema can be—and perhaps more importantly, implying that the often contradictory nature of beauty lies in the (camera) eye of the beholder.

The Radical Traditional

"I don't like change, I will always resist it, yet I promote it as well, that's the irony." Davies said this in 1992 (qtd. in Kirkham and O'Shaughnessy 15); the subsequent two decades seem to have only intensified this irony. Sixteen years later, in *Of Time and the City*, a film that is essentially about mourning for a lost paradise, Davies expends much of his narration bemoaning the perceived frivolousness of contemporary life—for instance, looking back fondly at the days before the tyranny of rock-and-roll, "when sportsmen knew how to win and lose with grace and never to punch the air in victory." Moments like these have instigated some critics to take exception to *Of Time and the City*, such as Ryan Gilbey, who wrote in *Sight & Sound*, "It's one thing for Davies to structure the film around his personal reflections on Liverpool, quite another to write off entire generations because they don't square with his view of society, pleasure, or progress" (47). Ambivalent though it may be, Davies's evident nostalgia for a bygone British era marked by severe social strictures, class and gender inequality, and draconian legal measures taken against homosexuals has been a source of harsh criticism against him.

At the same time, the filmmaker has often been saluted for positioning himself against the social and aesthetic norms of his national cinema. Tony Williams believes that Davies's autobiography-based work is more than merely introspective; it lays bare the truths of the repressive political regime from which it hails. Williams writes that *Distant Voices, Still Lives*, released during the height of the Margaret Thatcher era, "offers crucial insights into those insidious operations of gender conditioning that would eventually destroy the foundations of the British welfare state and led to Thatcherite hegemony" (246). Furthermore, Williams believes that Davies arrives at his politics through subversive aesthetic means, positioning him in a continuum of radical British filmmakers working against the mainstream: "Like Derek Jarman, Davies recognizes that an alternative British cinema must necessarily involve a different set of visual practices" (244). Michael Sicinski, writing for *Cinema Scope* online, has defined Davies in far more conservative terms, locating in his films the director's "quest for belonging . . . writ large as a social programme, an unreconstructed form of anti-royalist leftism that paradoxically favors the national social bond over the outlaw desires and discomfiting needs of the marginalized."

Clearly the politics of Davies's works are as defined by paradox as are his approaches to autobiography and his filmic technique, and they constitute a worldview that doesn't neatly align with socially acceptable ideas of liberal and conservative, left and right, forward-thinking and old-fashioned. How does Davies embody such opposed social perspectives within one uniform body of work? Is it possible that his filmography exists at the point where radicalism and traditionalism intersect? In the first part of this book, I attempted a definition of the content of Davies's cinema, based on an essentially anecdotal and personal history, concluding that the uneasy negotiation of his own personal trauma creates a queer form of autobiography, one that honors a repressive past while wrenching away from its grip. After that, I took a closer look at the strangely dissociative aesthetic created by this psychological split, and then ventured to explain how it is that Davies actually creates this world onscreen, marked as it is by a contradictory sense of joyful melancholy. With this grammar established, it now would seem beneficial to examine the ideological tenor of Davies's films—and try to trace the elusive social engagement of which the director partakes and then perhaps to define just how it is that Davies's work feels cinematically progressive while at the same time nurtures traditional values. The result of this is a narrative cinema that, in trying to break free from the complicated form of nostalgia to which it's bound, becomes strangely radical.

The first way to approach the conundrum of where to ideologically place Davies in his nation's alternative cinema is to acknowledge his awkward, difficult-to-define relationship to his country's tradition of realism. His initial films—the *Trilogy, Distant Voices, Still Lives,* and *The Long Day Closes*—were made in the long shadow cast by the films of the postwar Free Cinema documentary movement and the British "kitchen sink" dramas of the late 1950s and 1960s, movies that were popular and considered revolutionary when Davies was an adolescent and which are regarded as having constituted a New Wave. Free Cinema was the term Lindsay Anderson coined for a series of nonfiction films that were shown in a program at the National Film Theatre in the 1950s and positioned as radical alternatives to the British documentary tradition, which filmmakers like Anderson and Karel Reisz viewed as aesthetically unadventurous works of the establishment (with the notable exception of films by Humphrey Jennings). Free Cinema films such as Reisz and Tony Richardson's *Momma Don't Allow* (1956), Anderson's *Every Day Except Christmas* (1957), and Reisz's *We Are the Lambeth Boys* (1959) desired to bring an unprecedentedly unvarnished, almost anthropological realism to cinema, focusing strictly on London's working classes, whom the filmmakers felt had been marginalized by the larger cinematic industry. The New Wave films followed soon on their heels and featured many overlapping principal figures. Titles such as Jack Clayton's *Room at the Top* (1959), Reisz's *Saturday Night and Sunday Morning* (1960), Richardson's *A Taste of Honey* (1961) and *The Loneliness of the Long Distance Runner* (1962), and Anderson's *This Sporting Life* (1963) were widely praised for their vivid, unrelenting depictions of working-class domesticity and rage, and for what was perceived as an uncompromisingly bleak view of male-female relationships. These films—often described as "angry young man" movies—were fashioned as reactions to the polite "drawing room" tradition of earlier British style, as in *Brief Encounter* and the elegantly composed Ealing Studios satire *Kind Hearts and Coronets* (1949), both of which Davies has cited as inspirational; and their insistently grim black-and-white compositions were antithetical to the luxurious Technicolor palettes of the Hollywood melodramas and musicals on which Davies's cinematic love affair was formed. Purporting to offer a true picture of contemporary working-class England, the Free Cinema and New Wave films actually fit rather tidily into British cinema traditions, which has in various ways over the decades prized verisimilitude as the worthiest of aesthetic goals.

"The films of the late fifties and early sixties, which are now called kitchen sink, did seem rather revolutionary," said Davies. "But if you look at them now, you realize that they are drawn from the middle-class point of view. And they're relentlessly dreary. . . . Working-class life was difficult, but it had great beauty and depth and warmth" (qtd. in Dixon 189). Davies's take on these films, which were hugely influential to many filmmakers of his and subsequent generations, reveals that there was an essentially oppositional stance to his cinema from the beginning. Though Davies hailed from the precise social environment about which the kitchen-sink movies were allegedly telling the truth, or at least a version of a reality that flattered a certain type of liberal-minded moviegoer, he found them insufficient in reflecting the lives of those he knew. Because of his particular aesthetic sensibility, this did not mean that Davies would ultimately attempt to paint a "truer" or more authentic portrait of the working classes as he understood them, but that he would come at his brand of authenticity through idiosyncratic means, with fidelity only to his own memory and experience. Davies's early working life, for instance, would seem to mirror that of the protagonist in one of the more imaginative British New Wave films, John Schlesinger's *Billy Liar* (1962), whose stultifying job as a clerk in a grim London office cannot dampen his creative spark. The drabness of Davies's stifling office environment led him to more zealously pursue his artistic goals, whereas Tom Courtenay's Billy ends up stuck in his rut, much like the *Trilogy*'s Robert Tucker. Yet whatever kinship Davies could have felt with the characters in the kitchen-sink movies, his work does not reflect an interest in recapturing or furthering the style of the films in which they featured.

To properly understand what Davies was responding to when he started making movies, it would be helpful to discuss what it is that the new realist films of the late 1950s and early 1960s were themselves responding to. Postwar England was in the midst of an economic boom, with its citizens experiencing a welcome affluence following so many years of deprivation in the 1940s. It was a place and time where, as the British cultural studies professor Graeme Turner writes, "The revival of capitalist industrial production, the establishment of a welfare state, and the Western powers' unity in opposition to Russian communism were all inflected into a representation of a 'new' Britain" (38). Furthermore, between 1951 and 1964, unemployment was remarkably low, and prosperity was high. The Conservative party was in power during this entire period, and its continual defeat of the Labour party, plus the alleged ascendance of the working classes into the middle class, made those in power seem untouchable. The received narrative of the period, then, was that the old class barriers were dissolving in the face of this new affluent society. Of course, such widespread political optimism commonly masks harsher realities. As John Hill writes, "What the rise in incomes and apparent abundance of consumer goods disguised then was the fragile and temporary base upon which such 'affluence' had been secured. Moreover, what it also disguised was the persistence of inequality in the enjoyment of 'affluence' and its continuing complicity with a structure of class division" (9).

At the same time, a newly emergent British youth culture was being sold more commodities than ever before, and thus the teenager was ascendant as a credible social being fully engaged in a capitalistic system. This reality, along with the public's just-below-the-surface awareness of society's continued inequalities, made for a combustible mix, leading to an explosion of vibrant, vital, youth-targeted film, theater, and music in the late 1950s. For British cinema this was viewed as particularly imperative, as many felt that the medium had lost its bearings. According to Charles Barr, "Cinematically as in other ways, the postwar years were to be perceived as a steady process of disappointment and anticlimax, a falling off from a lost Golden Age of purposeful austerity" (13). By the end of the decade, long gone were the glory days of instant classics such as *Brief Encounter*, conceived and produced in the shadow of the war; the heyday of the John Grierson and Humphrey Jennings films, made in the documentary-realist tradition which had given the national cinema its noble identity, was also very much in the past. The arts were ripe for a shakeup, although the revelation would manifest as a newly unrefined form of realism that prized the raw and the adversarial.

A first major moment of impact—one that helps to define and further complicate Terence Davies's relationship to this era of popular culture—came via the playwright John Osborne's transformative *Look Back in Anger*, which electrified the London theater world in 1956. An excoriating take on contemporary British living from the point of view of disaffected, working-class Jimmy Porter, ranting and railing against the powers that be and his wife's upper-class family from his dismal one-room attic flat in the Midlands of England, Osborne's play all but defined and initiated the character of the "angry young man."[5] With its unapologetic sensuality and rage, *Look Back in Anger* at first perplexed critics and audiences, but buoyed by the ecstatic review of the influential *Observer* critic Kenneth Tynan, who dubbed it "the best young play of its decade" (Lahr 13), the show was summarily recouped as a corrective to what was seen as a staid British theater tradition, of which the playwright Terence Rattigan was deemed a prime culprit. Rattigan was held up as an exemplar of unfashionability; his buttoned-down, sexually repressed characters were the antitheses of Osborne's raging extrovert. Such plays as Rattigan's *The Browning Version* (1948), *The Deep Blue Sea* (1952), and *Separate Tables* (1954) were thus viewed as symbols of the old guard. That their stiff-upper-lip politeness masked profound ruminations on social and sexual torment mattered little to the purveyors of the new movement, for whom the "angry young man" plays felt like an emotional prison break. What's more, Rattigan explicitly positioned himself against anything that was taking theater in a radical direction. According to Dan Rebellato, "Rattigan decried the new movements, Beckett and Ionesco's turn from Naturalism, the wild invective of Osborne, the passionate socialism of Wesker, the increasing influence of Brecht" (xxi). Rattigan fell far out of favor, and his 1960s work was regularly panned for allegedly being out of touch. Yet as Davies said in an online interview in 2011, when discussing what he perceived as the continued relevance of Rattigan: "The irony is that you read *Look Back in Anger* now and *that* looks like the antique play" (Bibbiani).

That Davies would eventually adapt *The Deep Blue Sea* into a film on the occasion of the playwright's centenary doesn't by itself indicate that he would align himself more with Rattigan than the artists who were reacting to Rattigan. But the kinship between the two is apparent, from the struggles both had with their homosexuality to the bedrock of British decorum upon which their works are grounded and which they subtly deconstruct. Furthermore, Davies has spoken of his admiration for the films of both *The Browning Version* (1951) and *Separate Tables* (1958), while all but disavowing the kitchen-sink realist films as contrived: "What is sad about them is that there isn't an ounce of sentiment in any of them" (qtd. in Dixon 189). Nevertheless, Davies's cinematic approach to gayness and sexual repression is entirely different from that of Rattigan, who was more bound by the strictures of his time. Many of Rattigan's plays, especially *The Deep Blue Sea,* were viewed as veiled accounts of homosexual characters, though Rattigan, who was known to be gay but who would remain semi-closeted throughout his career, routinely denied the charge. Davies's films show no evidence of sublimation. Desire is on the surface, as is evident from the shower scene in his very first film,

Children, to the remaining films of the *Trilogy*, which similarly do not shy away from intimations of same-sex desire and eroticism, despite their distancing layers of trauma-induced guilt.

Today, queer cinema has come to be regarded as a subgenre unto itself, yet Davies's films—made before the term was coined in the early 1990s—are hardly, if ever, retroactively snuck into this niche. In 1998, when asked by B. Ruby Rich what the ideal queer film should be about, the important gay British filmmaker Isaac Julien responded, "about the family, because that is the great unspoken subject in queer culture, the site of trauma that no one has talked about" (44); as the family and childhood as a site of queer trauma is arguably one of Davies's most interrogated zones, Julien's quote goes a long way in expressing how ignored Davies's work has been. The closest compatriot he might have in the queer-cinema canon is the late Derek Jarman, a British director born three years before Davies, whose most influential features were produced during the same era, and which take their aesthetic cues liberally from classical European portraiture, American beefcake photography of the 1950s, and the 1970s punk style. Jarman's first feature, the unabashedly homoerotic and stylized *Sebastiane*, concerning the martyrdom of the title saint, was made in 1976, the same year as Davies's *Children*. Davies and Jarman have occasionally been spoken of in the same breath by critics and film scholars, especially as they became symbols of a new wave of British filmmaking in 1980s England, yet their levels of explicit political commitment as artists vary considerably. All queer films are by nature oppositional, functioning as alternatives to heteronormative Western moviemaking practice, but not in the same ways. While Armond White argues that Davies's work is "structured around the subtle, circumspect subversions practiced by oppressed groups—women, specifically, but by extension, gays, the working class, and so on" (134), the political dimension of his films is somewhat diffused by the nature of their intentionally narrow perspectives. Davies has often acknowledged that he crafts his films through his own sliver of experience. Therefore, he looks back fondly at a time in his childhood not yet complicated by the vagaries and humiliations of adult sexuality, suffused with maternal tenderness and the togetherness and solidarity of an idealized working-class community. Davies's implicit longing for an age marked for him by traumatic puberty, and for generations of gay men by closeted, criminalized desire, makes him a tricky figure for politically viable queer appropriation. Contemporary film and television images of homosexuality are ideologically burdened, encouraged to wear an imprimatur of social pride and ignore the tortured past; Davies's agonized psychological portraiture, which originates from a place of entrenched sexual mortification and disappointment, thus seems doubly quaint. Yet to deny the grievances and suffering of former generations of gay men and women because the subject isn't trendy or politically expedient could be likened to historical amnesia; and similarly to refuse Davies the mark of important queer auteur is to imply that his unapologetically troubled response to his own homosexuality is invalid or, worse, somehow a symptom of social instability (which unexpectedly echoes the outdated, long-rejected notion that homosexuality is a mental disorder).

Davies's deeply personal brand of queer cinema is distinguished by an unfashionable notion: the impossibility of same-sex love and thus the tragedy of gay desire. But, crucially, the heightened artifice of his films set in a socially conservative period of British history reveals his self-awareness of his tendency to romanticize what has been lost and a sophisticated ambivalence about the past that he seems to regard with such reverence. As Sicinski argues, this makes for a complicated form of social conservatism: "Davies's cinema tends to posit a 'Britain' that exists only in his memories. Paradoxically, the fact that he never felt he could truly 'belong' there only made that world that much more perfect."

It just so happens that his idealization of the period squares with a strain of British cultural studies of the 1950s that derided popular culture. In that decade, writes Turner, "The mass culture of contemporary England was unfavorably compared to an earlier, albeit mythical, folk culture located in some past formation of the 'garden of England'" (54). The theoretical and critical purveyors of this point of view, such as Richard Hoggart and Raymond Williams, were hardly traditionally conservative but rather left-wing champions of the working-class; it was the loss of the underclasses' rich culture they were bemoaning in the face of industrialization and modernity. Cinematically, their perspective was most in line with the Free Cinema purveyors, whose films, according to the critic Andrew Higson, evince an "anxiety over the erosion of traditional, organic culture by mass culture. . . . They seem also to pose the question of whether the newly emergent perception of 'spontaneous youth culture' [the jazz club in *Momma Don't Allow*] has come to replace the traditional forms of working-class culture as the site of 'real,' 'authentic' cultural values" (91). These fears were not alleviated in the 1960s, when British pop exploded throughout the world, drawing attention to "swinging" London's mod fashions, James Bond movies, and, of course, the Beatles, who hailed from Davies's hometown of Liverpool. In this way, Davies's snide dismissal of the mop-topped superstars in *Of Time and the City*, whom he likens to "a firm of provincial solicitors" and whose song "She Loves You" he mocks in voiceover imitation, is in keeping with an established thread of liberal-minded social commentary. Nevertheless, as the years have worn on, the seeming traditionalism of Davies's perspective puts him at odds with contemporary liberal politics, even if his cultural alignment with outsiders—the working class, women, gays—would seem to place him firmly to the left.

What most complicates charges of Davies's conservatism, however, is the nature of his cinema itself. His films' textures, structure, and audience address are wholly outside of mainstream trends and discourse. His films may not be thematically oppositional, but they are undoubtedly confrontational in style and tone. If one can define what is traditional about Davies's point of view as it is reflected in his cinema, then one also needs to understand what makes it radical. Aligning him with the nontraditional Scottish filmmaker Bill Douglas, known for his harrowing, spare films about growing up in an impoverished mining community in Scotland, John Orr claims that Davies's films constitute "an alternative strand in British film history to the studio legacy of Michael Powell which has clearly influenced [Davies's cinematic peers] Peter Greenaway and Neil Jordan" and that they "seem impossible to imagine without the emotional intimacy of Bergman or the complex memory narratives of Resnais and Fellini" (47). Such comparisons to directors commonly recognized as art filmmakers—in other words, whose films function outside the industrial mainstream—are not uncommon in discussions of Davies. But it is perhaps more important to note that those references exist comfortably alongside Hollywood and British studio films as well, when trying to define Davies's visionary cinematic identity. Adrian Danks wrote of *Distant Voices, Still Lives*, "A film which can, in turns, effectively evoke the cinema of Michael Powell and Emeric Pressburger, Bill Douglas, Yasujiro Ozu, and the MGM musical must be considered in terms that respect its cinematic specificity" (53). That Davies has been considered both kin and counterpoint to British cinema's patron saint of audacious artfulness, Michael Powell, speaks well to his complex aesthetic, and that Davies's films evoke both the stringent, existentialism of Bergman, according to Orr, and the Technicolor glory of the Hollywood musical, according to Danks, marks his films as peculiar hybrids. In his book *Essential Cinema*, Jonathan Rosenbaum reaches further in his evaluation of *Distant Voices*' stylistic paradox: "Technically speaking, Davies's film is closer to the avant-garde, but its emotional impact bears more relationship to directors like John Ford, Yasujiro Ozu, Robert Bresson, Charlie Chaplin, Kenji Mizoguchi, and Leo McCarey than to any experimental or realist contemporaries of Davies that come to mind" (388).

The crucial radicalism of Davies's art, then, comes from the way he synthesizes his twin tendencies, to both embrace and reject the emotional directness and artificiality of traditional forms of industrial filmmaking. At the beginning of his career, Davies's aesthetic may have been what one might more commonly refer to as that of "art cinema," as evidenced most prominently by the extended single take that records Tucker's bus ride with his mother in *Children*. The immobility of the camera as it watches the mother in profile, her face slowly crumbling in despair over the course of two punishing, uncut minutes of screen time, would seem to place Davies within a tradition of "durational" art cinema, some of the most celebrated stylists of which include the avant-gardists Michael Snow and Chantal Akerman, of Canada and Belgium, respectively; the Iranian filmmaker Abbas Kiarostami; the Hungarian Béla Tarr; and the Taiwanese Tsai Ming-liang. And while Davies has continued to shoot extended takes throughout all of his films—for artistic and economic reasons—the insistent focus, silence, and austerity of *Children*'s bus scene places it an entirely different context, one that has no equal in his filmography. Rather, Davies's aesthetic has grown more difficult to categorize, imbued as it is with not only elation and misery in equal measure, as discussed in this book's prior section, but also avant-garde and Hollywood tendencies.

He accomplishes this not through simple homage, but rather by becoming a distinctly queer reappropriator of a very particular era and category of popular culture (forties and fifties Hollywood, big-band music and American songbook standards, broadly). By taking preexisting pop-cultural elements and reintegrating them into aesthetically dissimilar contexts, Davies creates a jarring and wholly original form of filmic collage; in it, the pop-cultural past is also a return of the repressed, at times inseparable from the pain of abuse, torment, and loneliness. Not entirely dissimilar from a camp aesthetic—which is identified by its preoccupation with trauma and outmoded elements of popular culture—this is perhaps the clearest evocation of Davies's eclecticism. As Elizabeth Freeman writes, this form of art-making, of "dragging a bunch of cultural debris around us and stacking it in idiosyncratic piles *not necessarily like any preexisting whole,* though composed of what preexists," is something of a hallmark in queer artistry (xiii). In Davies's dazzling construction, mainstream popular signifiers—including Nat King Cole and Jo Stafford songs as much as classical Hollywood movies—are rendered fresh and strange, existing outside of the dominant, heteronormative culture, and the films containing them bold and unconventional and outside of the commodified entertainments that historically housed them. This constitutes Davies's most radical tendency—ironic for an artist who flat-out rejects the turning point in popular culture when artists such as Elvis Presley and the Beatles were reappropriating earlier forms (folk music, black culture) as well.

I would argue that such an approach puts Davies's films in line with those of the New Queer Cinema artists of the 1980s and 1990s he is not normally categorized with. B. Ruby Rich's working definition of these films would seem to at least aesthetically encompass much of Davies's work. She wrote in 1992, the year *The Long Day Closes* was released, "The new queer films and videos aren't all the same and don't share a single aesthetic vocabulary, strategy, or concern. Nonetheless, they are united by a common style: call it 'Homo Pomo.' In all of them, there are traces of appropriation, pastiche, and irony, as well as a reworking of history with social constructionism very much in mind" (18). However, she goes on to complicate our positioning of Davies here by also insisting that the New Queer films are and therefore must be "irreverent, energetic, alternately minimalist and excessive. Above all, they're full of pleasure." Such exclusionary measures toward a working definition are undoubtedly and understandably political, accepting appropriation and pastiche as hallmarks of a new gay cinematic movement, as long as the entire package is justified by a rhetoric of pride. Where this leaves not only Davies's work but also such dark-tinged concurrent New Queer cornerstones as Tom Kalin's *Swoon* and Todd Haynes's *Poison*—complicated negotiations with queer history and identity interested in much more than mere visibility—is unclear. Regardless, Davies's cinematic approach, however or wherever one slots it into received notions of an acceptable queer aesthetic, reflects a remarkably personal evocation of identity, desire, and loss, opening up rich avenues with which to explore historical notions of queerness.

Davies's artistry and identity are clearly by-products of his all-consuming movie love. As he states in his narration for *Of Time and the City*, at seven years of age, he "discovered movies and *swallowed* them whole." The notion of Davies having not only watched films but ingested them, crucially at a presexual age, articulates the way they resurface onscreen in his work. Davies's continual return to these moments of prepubescent joy reflects a nostalgia for a time when the object of his desire was necessarily abstract, uncomplicated by the perception of unwholesomeness. In retrospect, however, adulthood's reality and disappointment imbue these images with a crucial difference. More narrative-based alternatives to the works of Anger or Warhol, they at once demonstrate a buoyant love for movies and a skepticism about their healing powers as entertainment. Matthew Tinkcom could also be describing Davies's work when he writes in *Working Like a Homosexual: Camp, Capital, Cinema*, his study of queerness and camp in mainstream cinema, that Warhol's films "gain their experimental excitement because they are dialectically situated in response to Hollywood; rather than choose to ignore the presence of studio production in the shaping of consciousness and representation, Warhol's films embrace and interrogate Hollywood" (74).

For Davies, not only movies but also the psychological *traces* of movies become cinematic layers. Sometimes this is accomplished simply through direct visual or aural reference, as in the appearance of the one-sheet for *The Robe* at the opening of *The Long Day Closes*, or when Eileen and Maisie attend a screening of *Love Is a Many-Splendored Thing* in *Distant Voices, Still Lives*. Yet the way Davies goes on to weave the reference of that 1955 Jennifer Jones–William Holden melodrama into the film's overall tapestry shows his idiosyncratic artistry. As the sequence begins, we see an exterior shot of a cluster of umbrellas in the pouring rain outside a movie theater. The camera cranes up, past posters for *Guys and Dolls* and *Love Is a Many-Splendored Thing*. When we cut inside, Davies cues to us that the film showing is the latter, not because we see the screen, but because an instrumental rendition of Sammy Fain's theme song for the film overwhelms the sound track, and from the wet cheeks of the hankie-clutching sisters it is clear that they are watching a tearjerker rather than a giddy gangster musical. At first, the scene skirts nostalgia and potential parody, as the exaggerated emotions of Eileen and Maisie and the quaint image of a theater filled with curls of cigarette smoke firmly place the scene in an alien past. But the intense, hyper-emotion of the women and the heightened drama of the swelling music is complicated by a sudden, intrusive cut. Though Fain's score continues to crescendo, Davies now presents us with a strange composition that is at first difficult to make sense of: two symmetrical rectangles of light, made up of grids of small windows, surrounded by darkness so that they appear to float in midair. We soon realize that we are looking down at them from a ninety-degree overhead angle, as two male bodies enter the frame in freefall. In slow motion, they tumble vertically through the air, away from the static camera, until they reach the windows, at which point they break through the glass, which shatters into countless tiny shards. The men continue to descend, the blackness underneath enveloping them. The music comes to an end with this sudden shock of decontextualized violence, which exists in an incomprehensible time and space when we first see it.

As the next scene, set in a hospital, shows, this was a poetic evocation of an on-the-job accident suffered by Tony and George, Eileen's husband. It was based on true incidents from Davies's past, experienced by his brother and sister's husband, though temporally altered; said Davies, "Those were two separate accidents. But dramatically, two separate accidents are not interesting" (qtd. in Farley 16). In presenting this memory in this place in the film, Davies has effortlessly created a bridge between two disparate spaces—the emotional, womblike fantasy of the movie theater and the harsh reality of the working world, the feminine and the masculine.[6] But he has also defamiliarized the well-known Hollywood classic's sound track, repurposing its tone and overblown sentimentality to express something dark and destructive that undergirds the sisters' experience. The theater is revealed as a false escape, and thus working-class life as precarious. The floor beneath is waiting to give way at any moment.

Tragedies imagined and real
in *Distant Voices, Still Lives.*

Movies are not complete entities in Davies's films; they are remnants of lost objects. The process by which Davies forages through the past and stitches together its remains is not merely a way of reclaiming or sharing these memories in an artistic context. It is a way of repurposing them into something *else*—something closer to utopia. The most remarkable sustained example of this in Davies's career is undoubtedly *The Long Day Closes*. Like *Distant Voices, Still Lives*, its logic is beholden to nothing other than the associative memories of its maker, but its nonlinear collage is not only made up of familial remembrance. It is a roiling stew of consciousness, and what often bubbles to the surface is movie detritus, snatches of dialogue or song that have been floating around in Davies's (and implicitly Bud's) head for years. The radically dissociative aural component of *The Long Day Closes* is its most disconcerting quality—often the film feels more like an abstract audio installation than a narrative movie.[7]

Davies begins the film with an agglomeration of images and sounds that thoroughly upend traditional narrative-cinema viewing methods. After the film's credits, we fade in on a most unexpected first shot: a gray brick wall in tight close-up, an image of closure and claustrophobia rather than the broad opening-out we normally associate with beginnings. Stranger still, when Davies dissolves from the title sequence to this image, the accompanying sound is the banging of a loud gong, with the constant pour of rain layered underneath it. Viewers of British cinema of the 1940s and 1950s may recognize the sound from the introductory logos for the famous J. Arthur Rank Organisation, the studio behind such films as *Brief Encounter, Great Expectations* (1946), and *The Red Shoes* (1948): all kicked off with the image of a bare-chested behemoth hitting a gong, a world-famous emblem of a particular national cinematic era. After this, we hear a voice floating over the sound track saying something odd: "A tap, Gossage, I said a tap. You're not introducing a film." Though it is never explained, this is the voice of the legendary British actress Margaret Rutherford (one of Davies's favorites, often invoked in interviews) in an early scene of Frank Launder's light boarding-school satire *The Happiest Days of Your Life* (1950), which Davies placed on his 2012 top ten favorite films list in *Sight & Sound* (63). And immediately following this, there emerges a familiar tune of rattling drums and blasting trumpets: Alfred Newman's triumphant, bombastic Twentieth Century-Fox fanfare, the musical theme that has launched decades of Hollywood mega-spectacles. We're used to hearing it while seeing the accompanying visual of the studio's name in colossal font surrounded by searchlights. Here, all we see are these drab slabs of brick. The gap between what we're seeing and hearing is immense, preparing the viewer to engage with the material in an entirely new way. Rutherford's comment—an offhanded remark her schoolmistress character makes to an underling who hits a small gong too loudly, clearly intended as a metatexual reference to the Rank logo—makes little sense if one hasn't seen *The Happiest Days of*

Your Life. And unyoked from the images that traditionally accompany them, the Rank and Twentieth Century-Fox soundtrack introductions become both immaterial and symbolic, creating an aesthetic rift in the film's fabric right off the bat—*The Long Day Closes* is a production of neither studio, which heightens the surreality of these logos, signaled only aurally. At the same time, their invocation ironically comments on the grandiosity of conventional studio-financed movies, their promise to whisk viewers away to fabulously exotic worlds, places that require introduction by a blast of trumpets or the strike of a gong.

With the first camera movement, Davies intimates the reality behind the dream. Davies cranes down, revealing a poster of the Twentieth Century-Fox biblical epic *The Robe* (a touchstone of the director's youth), as well as a street sign revealing the name of Davies's childhood street, Kensington, before panning right and holding on a view of a rain-drenched, abandoned alley. With slow, deliberate movements, the camera creeps forward as the verse to Nat King Cole's "Stardust" comes in; through the rain, the camera eventually swings right and dollies into a ramshackle, boarded-up row house's front door. Brief silence on the sound track is followed by another piece of decontextualized dialogue that functions as a free-associative verse for Davies, this time spoken by Alec Guinness in Alexander Mackendrick's *The Ladykillers* (1955): "Mrs. Wilburforce, I understand you have rooms to let." Finally, after a cross-dissolve, the rain stops, the sun comes out, and we're now in the past, as the same house stands before us inhabited and in working order; here we meet Bud for the first time, perched on the staircase and asking his mother if he can "go to the pictures." As an introduction to a character, this opening sequence is unusual; as an establishment of setting, it is downright radical. The camera's gaze and movement emerge from no established point of view, creating a free-floating atmosphere that prioritizes omniscience over subjectivity—especially disorienting in a film framed as personal recollection. Despite the scene's essentially gritty setting, we have entered a strange netherworld that exists exclusively in the memory of the filmmaker, a liminal space that neither reflects a recognizable reality nor retreats into fantasy.

Many of Davies's films do not conform to the linear standards and codes of classical narrative because they are too preoccupied with time and memory. Yet they are not beholden merely to flashback; rather, works such as *Distant Voices, Still Lives* and *The Long Day Closes* create highly unorthodox filmic spaces where the expectations of narrative are made subordinate to the vicissitudes of the ever-present past. One memory leads to the next in an endless looping of seemingly disconnected sequences that function on an internal logic. As expressed in this opening, all of *The Long Day Closes* is marked by an experimental free-association: the film is woven together not simply with concrete, visually evoked memories but also with snatches of audio from such films as *The Magnificent Ambersons* (1942), *Meet Me in St. Louis* (1944), *Carousel* (1956), *Great Expectations*, and more, employed as barely perceptible echoes of the child's and the filmmaker's pasts.[8] The clips reflect Davies's fears as well as his fond memories; speaking of the film's aural landscape, Colin MacCabe told me in an interview, "You could kind of psychologize it, and say that it's Bud's unconscious . . . these sounds are the fundamental ways in which he interprets his reality of these Hollywood films. *The Magnificent Ambersons* is there as decline and decay. I think Miss Havisham is there as a terrible vision of what his life is going to be." Because these moments are often linked more to an omniscient authorial perspective than a specific character's recollections, Davies is able to represent free-associative, stand-alone images that function as both individual recall and cultural reference points that trigger the viewers' own memories. And since narrative chronology is not the goal, Davies can indulge in the odd cinematic flourish without stopping a film in its tracks.

The Neon Bible offers one of his most memorably radical gestures. "I didn't want to dramatize the book . . . I wanted to interpret it," Davies has said, which goes a long way toward explaining the film's odd sensation of purposefully stalled dramatics. Rather than lay out the novel's events in a traditional cause-and-effect manner, he makes John Kennedy Toole's narrative markers into discrete elements that feel like isolated tableaux suspended in some eerie corner of someone's half-remembered past. Too diffuse to be a fully realized evocation of the protagonist David's personal story, and too foreign to Davies in environment to be seen as properly autobiographical, *The Neon Bible* is unmoored enough to roam free through its maker's subconscious. In one breathtaking moment, unhinged to character or even clear metaphor, Davies focuses the camera on a white sheet, hanging on the clothesline and flapping in the breeze. The shot comes soon after we discover that David's father has been killed in World War II, dramatized by David's mother weeping at the kitchen table over a letter that has informed her of his death and a shot of coffins draped in American flags. Davies has already created a feeling of emotional hollowness in this sequence, so when he cuts to the blank, colorless sheet, it reminds us of nothing more than a movie screen waiting to be projected upon. What is most thrilling and simultaneously disconcerting about the image is the music laid over it: the iconic, epic "Tara's Theme" from Max Steiner's *Gone with the Wind* score.

The juxtaposition of the familiar, exultant theme with a dissociated image of blankness is similar to the effect of the Twentieth Century-Fox theme over the colorless brick wall at the opening of *The Long Day Closes*. Both scenes call attention to film itself as a construct, a blank space onto which one can project triumph, despair, elation—any of which can be easily turned on or off with a switch. At the same time, it is another example of more traditional cinematic forms seeping into his films' unconscious and being radically defamiliarized: here *Gone with the Wind* makes for an awkward reference point. Both it and *The Neon Bible* are set in the South, but the similarities do not extend much further than this. Its recollection only imbues Davies's film with ambivalence. The invocation of the Hollywood epic, which takes place during the Civil War, might lead a more literal-minded viewer to draw parallels with *The Neon Bible*'s World War II setting, but its immediate emotional effect within Davies's film—and entire filmography—is rather subliminal. As the camera moves ever closer to that bedsheet, gently swaying but held tightly to the clothesline, and the music crescendos, one gets a sense of the ever-present past dominating blank spaces. The immediacy of the moment is thwarted by the events—the war and misery, perhaps, but also the songs, the movies, the poetry—of long ago. As I will discuss in the next section, the past is always present in Davies's films. We could view the sheet as time itself, a palimpsest on which the past is written over and over.

The Fixity of Forward Motion

Terence Davies's film of *The House of Mirth* begins and ends by explicitly situating us in a specific time and place. As it opens, with Lily Bart emerging from the steam of an arriving train in Grand Central

Station, we read the words "New York 1905" onscreen. At the end of the film, after Lily has fatally succumbed to a self-inflicted overdose of medication, and her beloved Lawrence Selden kneels by her limp body at her bedside, Davies captures them both in a freeze-frame—and as Alessandro Marcello's aching Oboe Concerto in D Minor comes to a poignant close, the words "New York 1907" appear prominently across the frame. It is a curious choice, but it has an undeniable emotional impact, the nature of which is difficult to ascertain. It is also a cinematically unorthodox decision: an opening marker is a common means of contextualization for the viewer, but a closing text card is unnecessary in this regard, its presence functioning in a distinctly emphatic vein, drawing the audience's attention back to time and place for a purpose that could seem more ideological, political, or perhaps philosophical. This audacious move was met with resistance: "I can't tell you the fight I had about that," said Davies. "Those two years in which it happened have got to be marked. . . . They're like emotional bookends, and I was determined" (qtd. in Everett 214).

There's something almost unspeakably affecting about these "emotional bookends." It is important to note that Davies talks about them in terms of time and not place—it was important for him that the *years* be marked. For a director who has always been particularly keen on unorthodox representations of time in cinema, this might not seem out of the ordinary, but there's something specifically moving and odd about Davies's reaffirming the period of time in which Lily's downfall is accomplished, and that the reminder that Lily's death occurs in 1907 appears over a freeze-frame (one that very slowly dissolves into white under the closing credits). One way to look at this is in broader social terms, as a reminder of women's subjugation in a metropolitan turn-of-the-century society that might consider itself enlightened, only thirteen years before the achievement of women's suffrage in the United States and the urban sexual revolution of the 1920s that would forever make the Victorian image of women like Lily a thing of the past. Lily's lack of options as a woman—born into privilege, taught little in the way of practical skills, and shunned for sticking to her moral and ethical principles—surely contributes to her fall from grace. But alongside a sociological reading, there is also something timeless in Davies's time-based gesture: a sense of stasis that rests uneasily next to an acknowledgment of mortality.

Lily's journey over the course of the 140-minute film—from wealth to poverty, from esteem to disreputability—is less one of devastating change than terrifying immobility. No matter her plans for progression, for marrying an eligible man, for making her own money through investments with Gus Trenor, Lily always finds herself back at square one. As Trenor reminds her when she refuses to submit to his sexual whims, she is "dodging the rules of the game"—yet if it is indeed a game, for Lily it is a zero-sum one, with no possibility for upward mobility. The nine thousand dollars Gus forces her to pay him back for his troubles is nearly the same meager amount of money that the otherwise penniless Lily inherits from her deceased aunt; her supposed windfall will go directly to Gus. It is upon absolving herself of this debt, quietly with two enveloped checks, that Lily overdoses.

For Lily, every move forward is a step back: even after being cast out of society, she is still financially beholden to it. Looking at Lily's life between 1905 and 1907 as a period of stasis, we might see her as already a ghost when she is introduced, ethereal and unsettlingly arch as she materializes from the fog of locomotive steam. Lily is therefore easily placed in line with Davies's other main characters, all of whom are in arrested states, paralyzed by the trauma of the past and stigmatized as social misfits. The most dramatic of these are the directly autobiographical figures: the *Trilogy*'s Tucker, stuck in cycles of repression and self-loathing from childhood to old age, his psychological trauma keeping him a prisoner of his own subconscious until his death; *Distant Voices, Still Lives*' Eileen, Maisie, Tony, and their mother, emotionally crippled by the shadow of the family's abusive patriarch even after his death. And in *The Long Day Closes*, the act of growing up is made to seem somehow impossible, as an ostensible coming-of-age portrait is gradually revealed as an expression that the experiences of adolescence keep one trapped in an amber of nostalgia forever, whether those experiences be painful or pleasurable. It is the opposite of a coming-out narrative—it's more like a crawling-in.

So consistently devoted to cinematically studying the nature of time is Davies that the title of his documentary *Of Time and the City* could only be slightly altered to fit many of his other films: we could call the *Trilogy* "Of Time and the Man," *The Long Day Closes* "Of Time and the Child," and *Distant Voices, Still Lives* "Of Time and the Family." Davies's films are shattering because time itself has been shattered—this ties his work equally to Deleuzian and queer theoretical concepts, as we'll see. In many cases, Davies inspects time by deconstructing it, telling his stories out of chronological sequence, as though the past itself is a broken glass vase whose shards have been reassembled into a free-associative mosaic of memory. The director has said, "I am obsessed with the nature of time and memory, and what gets me angry about films which are supposed to be about memory is that they're always linear. Well, memory isn't linear, it's cyclical and associative" (Concannon).

As I've noted, T. S. Eliot's *Four Quartets* is the central artistic touchstone for Davies's career, and its abstract metaphorical notions of time as a contradiction, as a giver and taker, healer and crippler, friend and enemy, are wholly in keeping with Davies's philosophy as reflected in his films. In a 2000 interview, the director implied that the *Trilogy, Distant Voices, Still Lives, The Long Day Closes,* and *The Neon Bible* somehow constitute an Eliot homage: "These were my modest version of the *Four Quartets,* based on the suffering of myself and my own family" (Hattenstone, "First Steps" 2). Eliot's cryptic, spiritually searching masterwork is a baptism that begins with roses and ends in fire; in between is an epic description of the eternal moment, detailing in a series of remarkable lyrical paradoxes that the past is never gone and that aging is itself not a progression. (Eliot's underlying message—and hope—in the poem is that the only release from time's constant trap is religious belief.) "To be conscious is not to be in time," writes Eliot, implying that each of our corporeal moments exists outside of traditional notions of temporality. And even as we move forward, ever closer to death, and our bodies ripen, wither, and finally fail us, we remain fixed in one point. In the third section, "The Dry Salvages," Eliot writes,

> It seems, as one becomes older,
> That the past has another pattern, and ceases to be a mere sequence—
> Or even development: the latter a partial fallacy
> Encouraged by superficial notions of evolution,
> Which becomes, in the popular mind, a means of disowning the past.

Eliot suggests that humans' fixation on progression and aging is tantamount to disengaging from and even rejecting the past, something that Davies would seem to agree with, if we use his films as evidence. "I don't see the past as a foreign country. I don't see it as having gone. I see it very much as a part of the present and future," said Davies (Fuller, "Summer's End" 55). Every moment in his films is a reckoning with the past, a reconciliation with the traumatic events that have created his and/or his characters' present. This is not accomplished in such simple terms as using flashbacks, which in films such as *Citizen Kane* (1941) and *Sunset Boulevard* (1950) are commonly linked to a specific subjectivity and provide textual psychological motivation. Rather, the past is a free-floating, all-consuming Now that often does not hew too closely to any one character's thought process, jumping back and forth as though on some imperceptible logarithm. For David Wilson, *Distant Voices, Still Lives* seeks "not so much to represent the past as time remembered, either with affection or with displeasure, as to render is almost as a present experience" (282).

In earlier sections of this book, I ventured to recoup Davies as a queer auteur, if a complicated one, in terms of the radical techniques he employs to aesthetically reconstruct his sexual identity via pop-cultural signifiers. Similarly, in his efforts to construct his own, reconstituted landscape of time in his films—a time that is so inextricable from his personal experience of the world—Davies creates a temporality that, in its unusual combination of stasis and motion, is as queer as his joyful-melancholy aesthetic. Contemporary queerness itself is marked by an inherent temporal stasis, eternally glancing to the stigmatized past for identification while gesturing to the future, with its potential for social progression. Davies's work, especially but not exclusively his emotionally painful memory films, seems to exist in the interstices of what we might consider the heteronormative everyday; whether the duration of a given scene is attenuated or abruptly clipped in order to drift to the next image (which often in "reality" exists prior to the image that came before it, or far later in the narrative before doubling back, but rarely directly following the former in perfect narrative chronology), it is firmly placed in its own temporal context, its own structure of emotional and social belonging.

In this final section, I will attempt to define Davies's portrait of time arrested as a manifestation of a queer temporality—in other words, one located outside the rhythms and punctuations of normal cinematic narratives and heteronormative experience. In Davies's case this is both because gay lives have historically been placed on what we might call an anticontinuum, an opposite track from the common definition of forward progression (queers are "branded as nonmodern or as a drag on the progress of civilization," as Heather Love writes [7]), and because Davies creates his own personal frozen time, as reflected in the narratives of antidevelopment that mark his most intimate films. Elizabeth Freeman writes of "queer time" in a way that eloquently illustrates the emotional tenor and political resonance of Davies's project: "I think the point may be to trail behind actually existing social possibilities: to be interested in the tail end of things, willing to be bathed in the fading light of whatever has been declared useless. . . . I find myself emotionally compelled by the not-quite-queer-enough longing for form that turns us backward to prior moments, forward to embarrassing utopias, sideways to forms of being and belonging that seem, on the face of it, completely banal" (xiii). Though Freeman is specifically writing about gay representation in art in the postrevolution 1970s and 1980s, her idea of queer art as existing at the "tail end of things" and thus forcing a search for meaning in "prior moments" is powerful, and clearly applicable to Davies's work.

In his films, the domestic space, historically the safest bastion of heterosexual tradition, is upended, fragmented, or made frightening; in *Madonna and Child* and *The Long Day Closes*, we only see a single mother keeping order of the household, while the limited scenes in *Children, Distant Voices, Still Lives*, and *The Neon Bible* in which both a mother and father are in charge of the home make for scenarios of violent uncoupling. Meanwhile, *The House of Mirth*, featuring an orphan protagonist residing in the home of her unmarried aunt, and *The Deep Blue Sea*, depicting the aftermath of a broken marriage, also firmly exist outside of the normal domestic sphere. All of his main characters, unmoored from familial and heterosexual romantic convention, would be declared useless by the dominant culture, and thus exist in their own realm; they are all put in the position of, following Freeman, trailing behind social possibilities, and searching for utopia—in Davies's case, often that is the past itself.

Another manner in which Davies communicates his films' and characters' placement outside of the normal social order is through his use of photographic tableaux. Earlier I touched upon how the influence of painting on Davies's aesthetic created an uncanny sense of cinema becoming a "still life," but if we momentarily disregard the painterly aspects of his cinematography that form the heightened reality of these frozen moments, there arises the question of their stillness and duration in relation to a psychologically motivated queer temporality. When we first see Maisie, Eileen, Tony, and their mother in *Distant Voices, Still Lives*, they are sitting stock-still, directly facing the camera—the three siblings are looking into the lens as though they are about to have their picture taken; the atmosphere, however, is funereal, and one would not assume the occasion for a group portrait. Nevertheless, this crucial introductory image inescapably reads as though a domestic photograph, and therefore signals two contradictions: a sense of inanimateness within a moving cinematic image, and a sense of normal household ritual that implies a "normal," linear familial landscape that the film ultimately rejects. The characters are trapped tightly within the frame, and thus are victims of Davies's stubborn, lingering past; even from the title, the film reads as Davies's boldest statement of the immobility caused by the lingering of past trauma. "The awfulness of the incidents it relates owes much to the stasis of the characters' lives, the compulsive repetition of the same injustices," writes Adam Barker. "Their lives are 'still' not just because they are past, but because they are predetermined from the beginning" (17). Such tableau-like images powerfully indicate Davies's need to arrest time, specifically the repressive time connected to his childhood. It is also important to note that within the film's opening photo-like composition, there is an actual photograph of Davies's deceased father hanging on the wall behind them—once the four people exit the frame, the camera tracks in on it for emphasis. For Phil Powrie, this arrested image indicates a "structuring trauma in the film's narrative, associated with the violent father, whom we see prominently placed in the background of the family pose as a photograph, both present as a spectral image and absent from the family group" (21). The father's absence-presence has an emotional grip on the living, making the home a spiritual holding cell.

Time and memory are the central preoccupations of Davies's career; according to Gilles Deleuze, they are the central preoccupations of film itself after World War II, as well. Therefore, it would seem imperative to place Davies's film within a Deleuzian framework, although this does not mean that we need to abandon evaluating it through a queer lens. Recently Nick Davis has called for a wider, more malleable approach to studying queer cinema that would allow its specific temporal conditions to be viewed in Deleuzian terms: "I argue for queer cinema as a Deleuzian minor cinema—a context that explains the troubles we find in naming, curating, or conceptualizing queer cinema as more than a cognate of LGBT filmmaking" (24). Davis's concept is helpful, pointing toward a definition of a queer cinema whose ruptures and amorphous images of desire are in part defined by a modernist temporal fracture, and in so doing releasing queer cinema from the burden of politics of positivity and identification.

In working toward an explication of a queer Deleuzian cinema, it is important to establish the basic theoretical concept of the medium itself, the only time-based art form other than music, as a means of capturing the essence and movement of time. What separates cinema from music, however, is its inherent ontological properties—its ability to visually record existence itself—as proposed most crucially in a bedrock work of film studies by André Bazin in the 1940s. In his essay "The Ontology of the Photographic Image," Bazin put forth a theory connecting cinema to its origins in photography, historically a medium for embalming, or mummifying, life. Photography and cinema are the ultimate expressions of the human desire for realism, which in this case refers to a need to capture man's essence; cinema takes it one step further, as the filmed image also implies the persistent, troubling reality of man's absence—the realization that life goes on unheeded in what is captured before the lens, namely, time and space. Wrote Bazin, "Now, for the first time, the image of things is likewise the image of their duration, change mummified as it were" (15). Andrei Tarkovsky's book *Sculpting in Time*, devising a theory of film based on the director and screenwriter's own working methods, furthers this Bazinian notion: "Cinema came into being as a means of recording the very *movement* of reality: factual, specific, within time and unique, of reproducing again and again the moment, instant by instant, in a fluid mutability" (94).

Both of these approaches are based on an idea of cinema functioning within realist terms, of the image as a reproduction, however malleable. In *Cinema 2: The Time-Image*, Deleuze moved beyond this to identify a historical, technical, and perceptual split that occurred in cinema in the late 1940s, theorizing that cinematic images were no longer linked by rational cause and effect. Due to what he called a "break-up of the sensory-motor schema," Deleuze noticed "the rise of situations to which one can no longer react, of environments with which there are now only chance relations, of empty or disconnected any-space-whatevers replacing qualified extended space" (272). Here, what he names the "movement-image" (the use of images in succession to give the impression of movement or the illusion of movement itself—one example being the modern idea of cinematic montage) was suddenly subordinate to the time-image (an image that contains time itself in its purest state); thus, time no longer derives from movement, but rather the reverse. Duration was unbound to narrative forward motion. Deleuze proposed that this occurred, especially in the European cinema, partly because following the trauma of World War II, time and space have been severely disoriented, even upended, and the *present*, as it is revealed in a single image, is out of whack. What then occurs is a recapitulation of filmic time and space, within single shots and in the relations between shots, which often defies traditional notions of continuity. Time is thus perceived on film as a malleable concept, and cinema achieves something closer to thought processes than cinematic cause and effect. Deleuze goes on to write, "Recollection is only a former present, whilst the characters who have lost their memories in modern cinema literally sink back into the past, or emerge from it, to make visible what is concealed even from recollection" (xii).

It is provocative, then, to consider the films of Terence Davies, born in 1945, directly at the end of World War II, in terms of Deleuze's proposal. Davies's cinema is not only one of disoriented, fragmented time but quite explicitly about the defamiliarized spaces of the postwar British era. *Distant Voices, Still Lives* and *The Long Day Closes* both open with images of empty houses, awaiting the past to return and fill their lonely shells. In the opening of *Distant Voices*, the camera enters the row house, surveying a front hallway and staircase devoid of people but pregnant with meaning and memory; we hear but do not see Eileen, Maisie, and Tony, their footsteps echoing as they make their way down the stairs, their voices calling to their mother. The house is haunted by the memory of their presence. The effect is ghostlike, but even more uncanny than this, as our eyes and ears are not attuned to any one perspective; in analyzing this scene, Claus Christensen notes that "the spectator's primary identification with the camera as the one looking, is expanded into a secondary identification with the camera as *the one who is remembering*" (131–32). *The Long Day Closes* begins similarly, as the camera enters from a rain-soaked alley into the front parlor and staircase of Bud's former home, now dilapidated and boarded-up as though to ward off trespassers. In both cases, Davies soon cross-dissolves to an earlier time when the homes were full of life—following Christensen, it is as though we are privileged to witness the house's act of remembering. Davies's tendency to resurrect dead spaces returns dramatically in *The Deep Blue Sea*, which begins and ends with, respectively, dollies out from and into a charred husk of a house that is an evident victim of air-raid bombs during the war. We never find out who lived there—the camera meanders away and settles on Hester's rented flat a few doors down. In so intently focusing on spaces and structures altered by war and transformed by memory, Davies firmly situates his cinema in a Deleuzian realm, while at the same time establishing a free-floating psychological rationale for his disorienting reshufflings of time.

One might then view Davies's films in terms of the specifically queer Deleuzian suggestion by Nick Davis. He posits that for the queer cinema, the AIDS crisis is the historical catalyst, replacing World War II, that transforms and fragments the perception of time (9). Here, the catastrophe that ravaged and politicized the gay community is viewed as galvanizing cinema in a manner more radical than is commonly suggested about the New Queer Cinema—not only as an incitement to political engagement but as the cause of an exploration of style, form, and movement. This notion connects most clearly to Deleuze's theories of cinema as emanations of a postwar psychological state. Whereas Deleuze noted that pre–World War II cinema's experiments with time were mostly linked to "amnesia, hypnosis, hallucination, madness, the vision of the dying, and especially nightmare and dream" (55) in order to provide motivational phenomena, postwar filmmaking began to find little need for such explanations. Instead it became predicated on a free-floating anxiety that created an emotional estrangement between the self and the environment, and between time and place (as dramatized in films by Michelangelo Antonioni, Alain Resnais, and, in the more immediate postwar period, Roberto Rossellini).

As Davies's films have no clear structural rationale for their nonlinear shape outside of the traumatizing ghosts haunting their maker, it might be productive to view them in light of Deleuze's rendering of cinematic time and space and Nick Davis's fitting appropriations of those ideas; for a queer consciousness like that of Terence Davies, temporality is singularly out of whack. In the *Trilogy, Distant Voices, Still Lives,* and *The Long Day Closes,* the past intrudes upon the present in an uninterrupted stream, while in *The Neon Bible, The House of Mirth,* and *The Deep Blue Sea,* the past creates a different sort of fragmentation, initiating what could be read as a psychotic split between their main characters and the milieus they inhabit. *Of Time and the City,* meanwhile, synthesizes both approaches, taking as its subject the alienation Davies feels from the city of his childhood, now unrecognizable, and parceling out its musings in a poetic, achronological manner. In all cases there lies a paradox central to Davies's cinema, in which we are constantly being hurtled through the past and the present while his characters are always stuck in a fixed point in time. Discussing the conundrum of technically conveying this odd sensation in an interview, Davies simply asks questions, showing that he's still working through these issues himself: "If you dissolve, people know time has passed, and nobody has told them, they just know. How do you get over that sense of time passing, while sometimes making time feel suspended? Because as a child, you're not aware of time passing, it's as if you're living in the same continuum all the time, so how do you get over that?" (Concannon)

The palpable feeling of paralysis in Davies's films is remarkable because the director has proven himself particularly adept at conveying movement through time. *Distant Voices, Still Lives* is noteworthy for the way it records onscreen the progression of time, which is in some ways a natural by-product of its production, considering that the second half was shot two years after the first. This results in a verisimilitude of aging rarely seen within a single narrative feature, a subtly Proustian spectacle noticeable in Tony's added paunch or the ever-so-slightly visible fresh lines on Maisie's face. Davies poetically bridges the gap between the film's discrete halves with a lyrical sequence that is one of his most beautifully dreamlike passages. *Distant Voices* ends in stasis: an image of Mother surrounded by blinding white light, sitting in her armchair, sounds of the past echoing around her, including the violent screams of her dead husband, who remains visible in a framed photo on the wall beside her; then, the house at night, haunted by memories, Mother sleeping by the fireplace, the flames reflected on her face and the wall behind her—a comfort and a purgatory. *Still Lives* begins with the promise of change: Maisie tending to her new baby. In between, Davies conveys time's flow as though a stream of water in the River Mersey, with moonlight glistening on its undulating waves. The water proves to be a baptism of sorts, an attempt at starting over, as we then see a screaming Maisie in the throes of giving birth. Accompanied by the stirring melody of Benjamin Britten's 1930 choral work "A Hymn to the Virgin," this sequence visually and aurally evokes a drift across time and space—made all the more poignant by the reality that the family is caught in the folds of time rather than moving through it.

    Davies sculpts something similarly ethereal in a transitional sequence midway through *The House of Mirth*. It comes at a crucial point in the narrative, after Lily has been shamed and threatened by Gus Trenor in retaliation for rejecting his advances, and he has revealed the extent of her debt to him; furthermore Aunt Julie, condemning Lily's card-playing and perceived financial irresponsibility, has refused to lend her the money to pay Gus back. The next morning, Lily nervously awaits a visit from Selden, but Rosedale, who aided Gus in investing for Lily, arrives instead. Well aware of her dire financial straits, the wealthy Rosedale proposes marriage to Lily, making clear that it is above all a "business arrangement." She summarily turns him down. Literally overnight, Lily is well on her way to being a social outcast, disavowed by Gus (and by extension his influential wife, Judy), spurned by Aunt Julie, and denying Rosedale satisfaction. Here, Lily receives a phone call from the most malignant of her acquaintances, Bertha, offering a cheery invitation to vacation on her yacht in the Mediterranean. After she accepts, seeing it as a well-timed getaway from her travails, Davies dissolves to a later point in time in the same room, the furniture and chandelier now covered in sheets. The family has clearly left for the summer. Mozart's trio "Soave sia il vento" from his opera *Cosi fan tutte* drifts across the sound track as Davies tracks around the now-empty house, the white sheets giving everything a ghostly pallor, as though we're looking at a moneyed mausoleum—appropriate for a film that functions as one long, inexorable pull towards death. These images are reminiscent of Deleuze's consideration of the empty spaces and rooms in the films of a director Davies has often spoke of admiring, Yasujirô Ozu: "They reach the absolute, as instances of pure contemplation, and immediately bring about the identity of the mental and the physical, the real and the imaginary, the subject and the object, the world and the I" (16). Davies soon leaves behind these meditative interiors. The camera moves outside of the house, surveying the grounds, now swept with rain, and then hovers delicately over a lily pond in the backyard before gliding rapidly across its still waters; there is a dissolve, and the water seems wider, fuller, and sparkling—the sun has come out. The hull of a boat appears in the left corner of the frame, pushing forward through the water; with a tilt up, the camera reveals Monte Carlo in the distance, and, if we weren't already aware, we realize that Davies has transported us to the Mediterranean Sea with the airiest of techniques. This remarkable sequence is reminiscent of the one that bridges the divide between *Distant Voices* and *Still Lives* in that it conjoins disparate spaces and times with the promise of baptismal rebirth—but the past is not so easy to overcome. For Lily, the Mediterranean indicates an escape from New York, where her untrustworthy social circle is slowly conspiring against her; yet, as will be revealed, Bertha has laid an ambush for Lily, and her experiences on the yacht will only further lead her to doom. Davies's eloquent bit of time travel has only served to reaffirm Lily's entrapment.

The notion of growth and fixedness as existing simultaneously in the same action is expressed even more dramatically—in a single image—in *The Neon Bible*. Davies recasts John Kennedy Toole's coming-of-age story as an undoing; the book functions within the literary tradition of the bildungsroman, but Davies queers this, denying the story its natural forward progression, which would normally pivot on matters of psychological and moral growth. Throughout the film, the tension between what appears to be a straightforward narrative and the cinematic techniques that subtly obscure the parameters of that narrative—Davies's predilection for extended pregnant pauses, abstracted musical interludes, and shots whose duration goes past the point where most filmmakers would cut, all of which are highly unusual for the typically more sentimental American youth-recollection film—make *The Neon Bible* Davies's most quietly queer work. Its impenetrable stillness, so opposed to the narrative touchstones that demarcate "growing up," places it in close proximity with *The Long Day Closes*; there is an air of impossibility about David's maturity, a refusal to be redeemed by time or history that identifies his narrative as a distinctly queer one. There is no sense in the film that David is growing up in any conventional, or even positive, way. Davies's major stand-alone gesture to the child's sideways aging is a thoroughly odd, self-conscious visual effect in which David, while staring up at a full moon from his front porch, ages from tiny prepubescent to gawky, elongated teenager in one shot. His back facing the camera, David is pulled like taffy, his awkward transition into adolescence accomplished through a jarring technique that calls attention to itself as unreal. David thus literally grows, like Alice in Wonderland after she's taken a bite of the cake marked "Eat me"—but he stands literally in the same place, an indication of stasis amid physical development.

In adapting *The Deep Blue Sea,* Davies also frames his characters within temporal constraints; many of his visual choices—of people positioned in stultifying boarding rooms suffocated by wallpaper—highlight the shared, social past that haunts them. Each of the three main characters, Hester, Freddie, and William, is a study in stasis, immobilized by class, custom, and trauma. Even the film's structural circularities—it begins and ends on the same images; the plot occurs in one twenty-four-hour cycle; there is a consistent cascade of flashbacks that keep Hester in a perpetual twilight of the past—identify it as a work of terrifying stillness and immutability. While Hester is incapacitated by her era's expectations of womanhood and socially acceptable notions of desire, Freddie is a loner of a different sort, hobbled by the visions of death and destruction he saw during the war as an RAF pilot. Tom Hiddleston, who plays Freddie, described his character thus: "The war has left a hole in him that he is not prepared to look at . . . by the time Freddie comes to 1950, he is almost a man out of time" (qtd. in James 23). This manifests as social awkwardness, in terms of his readability and his ability to read others; he is given to unexpected outbursts followed by strange bouts of tenderness, all of it affected by nostalgia for the war, which has a terrifying stranglehold over him. A simple museum visit, for example, results in both distancing jokes about the painters ("Bric a Braques") and explosions of anger derived from his dissociation from contemporary culture. William, in contrast, is painfully reserved, a product of both a monstrous mother and a repressive society. He cannot even bring himself to fight Hester when he discovers that she has cheated on him and is leaving their marriage for the much younger Freddie; as played by Simon Russell Beale, William is a sculpture of propriety that one wishes to chip away at, his restraint clearly masking whirlpools of regret and disappointment. Together, these characters, according to Sean O'Connor, "represent a nation, bereft of status and Empire, crawling out of the wreckage of war into the light, but unaware of the future" (viii).

It's as though these three people—like Lily; and moving further back, like David and Aunt Mae; like Bud; like Eileen, Maisie, and Tony; like Tucker—are somehow asleep amidst life's ever-onward march, embodying Eliot's idea that "To be conscious is not to be in time." They live, but as ghosts, emanations from a past that will never die as long as they are conscious. They would all be at home in the rose garden that famously opens "Burnt Norton," the first section of Eliot's *Four Quartets*. The garden is imbued with inescapable memories, a place where spirits "dignified, invisible," move over dead leaves. One could say that Davies's gallery of characters constitutes his own Eliot-like rose garden, an enclosed space where nature and time take their physical toll, where flowers wither and leaves brown and crumble, but the past is always present.

Davies likens human experience to a transitory, rapidly decaying floral state in his opening credit sequence to *The Long Day Closes*. Seemingly branching off from Eliot's enigmatic, melancholy line, "But to what purpose / Disturbing the dust on a bowl of rose-leaves / I do not know," Davies presents as his first image a still life of a bowl brimming with red and white roses arranged on a table, illuminated by a shaft of sunlight. Unusual for the way that it presents the full cast of credits, normally saved for the closing scroll, this sequence—set to a minuet from Luigi Boccherini's String Quintet in E—is surprisingly lengthy, running a total of three and a half minutes. We may notice that, almost imperceptibly, the rose petals begin to wilt, an effect achieved through subtle dissolves. By the time the credits have concluded, with Terence Davies's name spread across the screen, fallen rose leaves are strewn about the table, though the image has remained completely, disconcertingly still. Even before the narrative has begun, Davies has situated his film neither in a specific place (the table's surroundings are bare, black, impossible to make out), nor in a particular period, but firmly *in* time. Even as time passes, dramatized by the decaying of the flowers, we

Time passing in the opening credits of *The Long Day Closes*.

remain suspended, fixed on what seems to be a single shot. Though the image records the passage of an unspecified length of time, its overall effect is one of immobility.

Davies makes us feel the minutes pass, forces an awareness of stillness. We are turned into active watchers even in our stasis. This is why this scene so uncannily evokes Eliot's mysterious line, "The roses had the look of flowers that are looked at." As though staring at a clock as its hands almost unnoticeably make their way around the dial, we are watching not simply a movie image but an encapsulation of time and therefore an expression of decay. Per Bazin, man's absence is as acutely felt as his presence.

Bathed in the Fading Light | 121

If we read this opening sequence as an expression of mortality, then *The Long Day Closes* comes full circle. At its conclusion, the film invites the viewer to consider both life and cinema in terms of their deterioration. In a moment of loneliness, a tearful Bud enters his ominous basement; as he's framed in the doorway, a deposit of coal cascades through the shoot to his left, creating an image of ashen despair. After we hear a melancholy yet decontextualized passage of dialogue from Orson Welles's *The Magnificent Ambersons* that, in its forbidding words, portends some form of incipient punishment ("George Amberson Minafer had got his comeuppance"), Bud enters an ominous door, all but dissolving into the black void beyond, unsettling sounds of staticky radio distortion accompanying his disappearance (in Davies's original screenplay, the disturbance is described as "the crackle of radio waves heard from deep space" [185]). From here, Davies adds another aural layer, an echo of Mr. Nicholls's school lesson on the properties of erosion, which the teacher divides into five categories: river, rain, glacial, wind, and marine. Though it is unsaid, all are agents of one larger category: time. "Life cooperates in the work of destruction," Mr. Nicholls instructs them, happening upon one of Davies's main themes. The physical destruction of time on the body as well as on human will is a central idea of *The Long Day Closes*; time marches forward, and it can leave us behind. As has been noted, Davies explains that this film, perhaps his most profoundly personal, is about a period of years—after his father's death and before the horrors of teenagehood set in—that were his happiest, and which came to a definitive end. Davies said about those years, "Everything seemed fixed and it was such a feeling of security that this is how it will be forever, and I really believed that; I didn't think I'd get any older and everything would stay like this forever" (qtd. in Kirkham and O'Shaughnessy 15).

After we hear Mr. Nicholls's lesson drifting across the sound track like some vengeful, whispering spirit from Bud's past, the camera rises out of darkness to reveal the backs of Bud and his friend Albie's silhouetted heads facing a screen. It appears as though they are in a movie theater, yet what is projected before them is not a Hollywood spectacle but rather an expanse of sky, with massive clouds slowly drifting across. The camera pushes into the screen, past the boys, until the image fills the frame. We hear chimes, and then the Arthur Sullivan–Henry Chorley choral song that gives *The Long Day Closes* its title begins, the entirety of which brings the film to its close. Davies holds on the image of the sun setting behind the clouds until it falls away, and the screen turns to pitch-black night.

At times, Chorley's lyrics cannot help but recall Eliot in their vivid description of time's effect on nature: "The last red leaves fall around the porch of roses / The clock has ceased to sound / The long day closes." As day turns to night, so does the sun set on Bud's childhood. By situating Bud in a space resembling a movie theater, Davies equates the process of erosion and the loss of innocence with the act of watching. For Davies, movies are memory, and therefore composed of moments ensnared in time's web. An expression of a past that never lets go, cinema itself is both saving grace and psychological entombment. The film leaves Bud immobile as ever, a boy on the precipice of adult sorrows, on the verge of a sexual maturity viewed as a betrayal rather than a becoming. He gazes ahead, a constant object while life swirls around him, a still point in the turning world.

Notes

1. The Toxteth riots occurred in July 1981, a violent incident in which members of Liverpool's inner-city black population rioted against mistreatment by local police.
2. Davies's assertion to me during an interview that the actors who played the middle-aged Tucker and his mother found the material "sordid" might also have had something to do with the ultimately reticent depiction of sex, which, of course, on film requires the participation of actors.
3. It is perhaps important to point out that Brambell was himself gay and did his best to keep this fact a secret for most of his career (Barrie, "Dirty Truth").
4. *Singin' in the Rain* appears on Davies's top ten list, included in the 2012 *Sight & Sound* poll of the greatest films of all time (Davies, "Greatest Films" 63).
5. Tony Richardson's 1958 screen adaptation with Richard Burton and Claire Bloom could only pale in comparison, even if it was among the first of the new social-realist films that would eventually take British cinema by storm.
6. *The Long Day Closes* furthers this bifurcation, as Bud himself seems to create a bridge between feminine and masculine spaces and bodies.
7. It is worth noting that Davies would ultimately write and direct two plays for BBC radio, the first in 2001 based on the third section of his novel *Hallelujah Now*, titled *The Walk to the Paradise Garden*; the second in 2007 adapted from Virginia Woolf's novel *The Waves*. Davies said in *The Guardian* in 2001:

"If there's a similarity between radio and film, it's the ability of both means of expression to concentrate on, and thereby highlight, small things to expose the intimacy, the poetry of the ordinary" ("Four Songs").

8. The rights to such a wide variety of clips for such a relatively low-budget film were largely secured by the composer and music producer Bob Last. Colin MacCabe told me in an interview on April 12, 2013 at the Criterion Collection offices in New York City that Last was "extremely canny at negotiating with Hollywood studios."

Interview with Terence Davies

The following conversation took place at Terence Davies's home in Mistley, Essex, on October 16, 2012.

MICHAEL KORESKY: I wanted to start by talking about T. S. Eliot's *The Four Quartets*. You've said it's the most influential piece of writing for you. One of its most haunting passages states, "Do not let me hear of the wisdom of old men, but rather of their folly / Their fear of fear and frenzy, their fear of possession." I'd like to hear how you feel about the poem now that you're older.

TERENCE DAVIES: I read them once a month, because I just love them. I think they're some of the greatest poetry written in English. When I first heard them, I was eighteen, I think. We had our first television, and over four nights Alec Guinness read them from memory. I had no idea what they meant at all, but I rushed out and bought them. And over the years, I've realized that the things I'm attracted to are the nature of time, the nature of memory, the nature of mortality, and the nature of the soul. And how small things, in memory and in real life, portray the greater truth. He also examines the way we perceive the world in a way I've only recently come to understand. Once we know we are looking at something, the object changes because we are aware of it. Most of the time we are not aware of it. "For the roses had the look of flowers that are looked at." Or: "Then the cloud passed and the pool was empty." In those moments, you're aware of the ecstasy of the moment, and even as a child I was aware that the ecstasy was going, it was going even as I was experiencing it. I felt that really deeply as a child; I didn't know what it was, but I felt it deeply. And I found that echoed in *The Four Quartets*. How do you come to accumulated knowledge? In the end is it really worth anything? Eliot remembers meeting a tutor from when he was being taught at university, and the tutor's basically saying, "All I've taught you doesn't matter. You've got to find your own language." But how do you find your own language? How do you find an emotional language? How do you come to terms with being in the world and then not being? I find that incredibly moving. It's influenced me in ways I hope I'm not aware of, because in that way, if you're truly influenced by something, then it comes out of you, but it comes out of you refracted.

The example I can give is actually music. If you hear Brahms's First Symphony, the big tune is exactly like the big tune in Beethoven's Ninth. If you hear the last movement of the Bruckner Ninth, it's like the slow movement of the Mahler Ninth. They're almost exactly the same, but they've come out refracted and different. When you're touched deeply by something, that in itself changes you, and you start to look at the world in a different way. Sometimes that can be very fulfilling, sometimes that can be very despairing. Because I think there's a lot of despair in *The Four Quartets*. There's even more despair in "The Love Song of J. Alfred Prufrock," which he wrote when he was *twenty-two*! It's not fair, is it? It's just not fair!

MK: You mentioned before about "finding your own language." Do you feel like after all these years making movies you've found your own language?

TD: No, I don't think we ever do, you see. It's the same as when I first started—just the fact that you were making a film was thrilling, and you did it on a little money. But now that feeling has gone. That's why

I don't go to the cinema much anymore. Because I can't suspend my disbelief anymore. Once you know how something works, it's very difficult to see the end product and have an aesthetic distance on it. 'Cause you're aware. You ask, Why are we tracking now? Whose point of view is this? If it's this person's point of view, why are we seeing scenes to which they're not privy? The quickest way to destroy something, especially a hobby, is to make it for a living. Occasionally, a film will come along and I'll think, Yes, this is a real proper film. Most of the time you watch the first two minutes and think, Oh God, I've got ninety-eight to go. It is very dispiriting, especially in this country, where we don't have an industry. It's a cottage industry. And we once did have a proper industry, where really interesting films were made, like, say, *The Pumpkin Eater* [1964]. It wouldn't get made now. No one would give you the money for that film now. It's a very good film, and Anne Bancroft is *wonderful* in it. I mean, *really* wonderful. I think she's even better in it than in *The Miracle Worker* [1962].

We don't have an industry, because lots of people don't see the difference between television and cinema, and there's a huge difference. Or we try to imitate America, which we do badly and we've always done badly. There's only one thing more embarrassing than an actor with a gun, and that's a British actor with a gun. They look *ridiculous*. And I just don't like this idea of all this quick cutting. You look at some of the great American films, and they're actually rather slow in comparison to films today. You're given the time you need. They cut it fast when they need to, and they cut slow when they need to. There's something really meretricious about it now, and I'm not interested in watching people shoot and torture one another. I don't want to watch violence. I had enough of that in my childhood. I want to tell these people, be in a room with someone who's violent just for a day. See what fun it is. It's not cool. It's not entertaining. It's really nasty. I know—my father was a psychopath. If I go to the pictures, and one scene of violence happens, I just go. I'm not watching it. It's like violence by proxy, a kind of thrill. And there's something drooling about it. It's not about film anymore; it's become about getting this man and this woman, and they get paid twenty-five million dollars to be in this film. This is not cinema, it's accountancy. And nobody's worth it anyway. I don't care how talented they are. Nobody's worth that kind of money. Perhaps cinema is in the process of dying. And if it does, it will be a great shame. It will be the only art form that arose, reached a peak, and died within a hundred years.

MK: If you say cinema is a potentially a dying form and that you've never found your language, and that when you watch movies you can't enjoy them because you see the strings, then frankly why do you continue to make movies?

TD: Well, I don't know. I wish I could answer that question for myself. I do want to do *Sunset Song*. And I want to make a film about Emily Dickinson because I love her poetry so much. I don't know why I do it now. One time I thought I knew. But now I don't know. How many people have seen any Ozu? Tiny amounts. That's dispiriting. That makes it harder to go on. Even though one should draw some succor from someone like Bruckner, who had only one success in his entire life. Most of his symphonies weren't played in his lifetime. I hope someone told him he was a genius, because he was. I don't know where he got the strength from. He was a devout Catholic. Perhaps his faith gave him strength. I am an ex-Catholic. I rejected it because it's a pernicious religion. But what do you put in its place? I did think that art of every kind was the thing that would fill that hole. But it doesn't always. I was rewatching Robert Hughes's *The Shock of the New* [1980], and he sort of comes to the same conclusion, that art can't change anything, that it can't pay your mortgage. Unless you're Brad Pitt. Then it could pay several mortgages—at the same time.

MK: So then perhaps the intent of making films is to bring something back to the form that you think has gone missing.

TD: When I was growing up, I think cinema was at its peak. I didn't start seeing things until I was seven, with *Singin' in the Rain,* my very first film, in 1952. But from about 1941 to late fifties, there's a glow about those films. It's opaque. I can't explain it; they've just got this glow about them. And cinema doesn't have that glow anymore, and certainly my films don't have that glow. And even the films that aren't very good, they've got a certain style. There's a film that was wildly popular in this country called *While I Live* [1947], and it's not very good—but the interiors are absolutely *sumptuous.* Not good, but stylish. That feeling we don't get now.

And a lot of those old cinemas are gone. So you're watching them in a box with a screen at the end. When I was growing up there were eight cinemas within walking distance of my house. And they were all different. I can remember where I saw certain films. Where I sat. The route I took. It was very powerful. That's gone now. We don't have that kind of cinema-going feeling anymore. Very often you stood in a queue. It was commonplace, because it was always full. I remember going to see *The Robe* [1953], and the curtains went back, and the audience gasped at the width of the screen. They literally gasped. That period has a wonderful glow. Just the way in which they're crafted. Like the opening of *All That Heaven Allows* [1956]: that first two minutes, you know exactly what the story is, where you are. It's just gorgeous. I was just recently watching *Shadow of a Doubt* [1943]. Everything is bathed in this glorious sunshine, but it's a very dark story. And with no strong black and whites; it's all this very soft sort of gray. It's got the most wonderful softness about it. Seeing again the other night *I Remember Mama* [1948], which was made in the forties. There are moments there that are so moving. *So* moving. When Oskar Homolka dies, and Irene Dunne just pulls the blinds down. Ah! That is an exquisite cinematic moment. You couldn't do it in any other art form. And I love that. *Letter from an Unknown Woman* [1948], even greater. It's just the incidental things. When she gets into his apartment and she goes to the piano. Do you know what the photographs on the wall are? They're of Brahms and Mahler. Mahler wasn't playing in the forties—or only in Holland. Someone took the trouble to do that. That interior is all sort of vaguely erotic, and it's just glass and wood. But the way in which it's perceived! I do miss that. Now they confuse prettiness with beauty. Because if something has meaning then you can shoot it on a knife and fork. It can be as beautiful as you want, but if it's got no emotional depth and you don't care about the people you're looking at, you might as well all go home.

MK: Though you speak of the beauty and luster of black-and-white, the *Trilogy* is your only black-and-white film. What was the decision for making those films in black-and-white, and had you ever considered making any of your other films in black-and-white?

TD: I was in drama school, and I'd sent off my little script everywhere, and it was always turned down, so I thought, It can't be any good. Anyway, I could afford to go home once every three weeks. And there was this program on BBC 1 on Friday nights called *Cinema Now*. And this particular Friday night, I got home and switched it on, and it was about the BFI Production Board. And so I sent them my script. And about three or four months later they asked me to go down to see them. They had a little office at the back of Waterloo Station. And Mamoun Hassan was running it then, a very brilliant man. He said, "You have eight and a half thousand pounds, not a penny more. You will direct." But when we were putting the little budget together, they said it's a color film, and I said, "No, it's black-and-white. It's a black-and-white subject." I felt that was right for the entire trilogy. Because the problem with color is that it does prettify and soften everything—there's an intrinsic richness you can't get away from. And I don't like pretty pictures. I think if the image has meaning, then it will be beautiful. But I always *felt* it was in black-and-white. And there was a lot of black-and-white footage in *Of Time and the City,* but I didn't shoot that, that was found. But there are just some films that *are* black-and-white.

MK: Did you consider making any of your subsequent films in black-and-white?

TD: No. We wouldn't have gotten the money.

MK: But would you have done it if money weren't an object? Were you scared of prettifying *Distant Voices, Still Lives*?

TD: No, because I think all the other films were color. I don't think they were black-and-white, but even so, just before we made *Distant Voices, Still Lives,* the last laboratory that processed black-and-white film closed down. So even if you wanted to make black-and-white you couldn't, because no one was processing it anymore. Obviously, in digital now they can just take all the color out. But you don't get black-and-white—you've got a film that has no color in it, which is different. But no, the others always felt color, but I always wanted to *do something* with the color. To try and get it as close to how I felt it should be emotionally. And we used the bleach-bypass process for *Distant Voices, Still Lives,* which had been used before: the first time it had been used was *1984* by Michael Radford. But the bias was towards blues and grays and reds, and my bias was to the spectrum of brown and pink. But I do think color has an emotional effect on you, so you have to be very careful when you use it.

MK: The color red is very important in *Distant Voices, Still Lives,* is it not?

TD: We do tests before any film, and we say that's the ratio, that's the color, that's the stock. Because you've got to find that out. We did a range of tests with this bleach-bypass process, which, if you just leave it as is, is really rather cold. And I didn't want it too cold. And we started to use coral filters and only occasionally putting gauze on the back of the lens to get the color that was important. And once we know what it's going to look like, we just shoot it. But the red lipstick and the red nail varnish—my sisters only ever used majestic red. It had to be majestic red, which was bright, strong red like you'd get in old three-strip Technicolor. That's what it looked like. To a child, anyway. And that process can make it go black or purple. So we had to watch that very carefully. So I said, "No, the lips have got to be red, the nail varnish has got to be red." That was a bit tricky at one point; now it wouldn't be difficult at all, as you'd just do it digitally. Back then it was a process that was just starting to be used; now they use it all the time. And you often think, why are we looking at this, what's it for? What they're doing now is *green*.

MK: You created your alter ego character of Robert Tucker [in the *Trilogy*], who grows from childhood to old age, when you were much younger. And you wrote a novel about this same character as well. I'm curious how you view the character of Tucker now that you're older.

TD: Well, I was at my lowest ebb when I was writing it and shooting it. I've always had the greatest difficulty accepting being gay. I don't like the gay scene at all. It was a criminal offense in this country until 1967, and when it started to open up a little bit more, and I went on the scene, I thought, I just can't accept this. Casual sex I just can't accept. I wasn't good-looking; no one was ever interested. So that's affected my reasons for being celibate and not practicing. But the *Trilogy* films were made when I was at my absolutely lowest ebb. I realized that Catholicism was a lie at twenty-two in the middle of Mass. They got to the offertory, and I thought, It's just men in frocks. I really did pray until my knees bled, and no succor came. And not that I watch my films anyway, but I certainly couldn't sit through the *Trilogy* again. It's too painful. And quite frankly, I don't know why people do watch it. It's terribly miserable—there's not a joke anywhere in it. It's really hard-going. I can't revisit that. My teenage years and my twenties were some of the most wretched in my life. True despair. Despair is worse than any pain.

MK: Though it is grim, I think one of the many reasons to watch the *Trilogy* is that it is technically virtuosic, especially for a film you made at a very young age. Can you talk about how you accomplished that extraordinary shot in which the father's coffin is being pushed into the hearse and the image of Robert and his mother at the window is wiped away?

TD: Well, this also involves serendipity. The shot was written as you saw it: that they would be seen through the hearse glass, and the coffin would wipe them off. It was a day like this [*gestures to the sunny day outside the window*]. What I didn't realize was that you'd have reflections on the top of the hearse. Which was pure luck. Because you then don't know where you are. That was *pure* luck! I couldn't believe it when I saw it. Because you're so concerned about getting the thing right with all those other reflections. It's the houses and windows opposite being reflected on the roof and on the glass. And that's sheer good luck. I never thought of all the reflections. Hearses are very shiny, obviously. It never occurred to me that there would be reflections. And the sun would have to be in the right place. I just thought, Haven't I been lucky?! God! [*Laughs*]

MK: That image is a zoom out. I'm curious if you see emotional differences between zooms and dolly or tracking shots?

TD: Well, I very rarely use zooms. Because then I didn't know the difference between a track and a zoom. I said, "Well, can we just come out from this spot?" And they said, "Well, we can't track because we're so close to the street." So I asked, what's the alternative? And they said, "You can zoom," and I said okay. As soon as I knew what it was, I knew that I would probably always track in the future rather than zoom. It has been used majestically—*Death in Venice* [1971] is an exercise in the use of the zoom, and ravishing to look at. We got away with it then, but in other situations, in other films, it wouldn't have been right. And I write it as I see it and feel it. I just do. And a lot of things that happened on *Children*, I just didn't know what I was doing. I just did it from what I felt was right. Which is how I antagonized the people working on it, except the cameraman. It was really the most unpleasant three weeks, to be told every day that it's lousy. And one time I fought back and said, "Well, if the script is so awful, why did you all say yes to it?" They all got quiet, in that British way. But I don't think I've used the zoom since, because it is an odd device. Because you're getting closer or further away from the subject, but you're not moving through space. And that makes a big difference. When something moves, *physically* you just feel different.

MK: There are so many shots in your films that look like paintings because of their beautiful sources of lighting in certain corners of the frame. Are you aware of this while you're shooting?

TD: No. I do love Vermeer, he's my favorite, but no, I'm not aware of it at all. Once you've discussed how it should look, then that's up to the cameraman. That's his job, and I won't interfere because I'm not technically minded at all. Once I know what it should look like, what's then important is the performance. You've got to believe the performance, because it can look as wonderful as you like, but if you're not involved, you're not involved. And everything's got to come down to it being true. But I'm not aware of it consciously. And I don't know much about painting. I remember when I was growing up, during school holidays, when you didn't have any money you just went to the pictures or go to the park, and we used to go down to the Walker Art Gallery in Liverpool and look at *The Death of Nelson*. That's a barrel of fun, I can tell you! [*Laughs*] I mean, I'd go nowhere else, I'd just look at *The Death of Nelson* and then go home. Absurd! Absurd! [*Laughs*] We looked at a lot of Singer Sargent before *The House of Mirth*, because he was the great portraitist of the belle époque. And you sort of forget it. But it's *there* somewhere. It's not conscious. I don't think it *can* be conscious. What's important is: is the shot true? Is the frame true? Is what they're doing in front of the frame true? If all those three things aren't there, then you really have a problem.

MK: What about that beautiful shot in *The House of Mirth* in which Lily is waiting for Selden, posed on the edge of the couch? The composition looks like a painting.

TD: Well, we found that house outside Glasgow. Because we shot mostly in Glasgow. And I found this old gentlemen's club, which was sort of ramshackle, and I said, "I think this would be really good for Aunt Julia's house." We did the stairwell and other interiors in another house, but this wonderful room was a billiard room, and that's where the ladies sat to watch the men play billiards. And that purple sofa was there—we didn't have to do it. We just put some new cushions down, and I said, "That's the angle we're going to see. That and the exit out of the room." We didn't have to dress the rest of the room. We just added some silks and some cushions. The wall behind was there; we didn't have to do anything to it.

MK: The waiting in that scene creates such a tension.

TD: When you're waiting for someone, even if they come a minute late, it seems like ten years. And what cinema is wonderful at is taking a tiny thing and making it long, and taking a huge thing and making it go like that [*snaps his fingers*]. And the emotional effect is very powerful. And if all you have is just stillness, and she's just waiting, that's all you need. And in those days, things didn't happen quickly. Life was slower. Because before she could take tea she would have had to put on a different dress. For every activity you had to have a different dress. Miserable! But if you get the stillness right, you can hold it for a long time. Even if you initially didn't think it was going to be like that.

MK: Similarly, in *The Deep Blue Sea*, you hold on Hester while she changes her dress to go out and follow Freddie. You just keep the camera there.

TD: But she got dressed really fast! I was really impressed! It was so wonderful. In my very first feature, in one shot he [Tucker] makes tea. Have you any idea the length of time to make tea? It takes years! I mean, whole civilizations could fall. It's coma-inducing! [*Laughs*]

MK: Well, I timed the shot of the rug in *The Long Day Closes*. Before the camera swivels, it's one full minute. At what point did you know that shot would be over?

TD: Well, it's because of George Butterworth's "A Shropshire Lad." Which is a set of poems by A. E. Houseman, which was then set to music by George Butterworth. And then he did an orchestral version. Oh, it's just wonderful. The tune is just fabulous. And I just thought we should time it so that the sun comes in and out and then we drift around it. And we did it, and I think that was the first take. God, it does last a long time! I thought once we put the Butterworth on it, it will hold. But people were furious. They either loved or absolutely *hated* it. One woman stood up and said, "Why are your films so bloody slow and depressing?!" and I said, "It's a gift!" [*Laughs*]

MK: Speaking of duration and letting things play out, how important is realism to you? British cinema has this tradition of realism, and your films often move away from that in many ways.

TD: I've always thought of it as just doing what is true. I can tell when something's not true. And that's even including the frame; sometimes it's just about moving it a centimeter. And what difference does that centimeter make? I can't tell you. I just know it needs to be here and not there. If it's false, the audience will know, and they'll know it instinctively. They may not understand what that is, but they know it. It's like certain actors come onscreen, and you can't feel sympathy for them. And it's got nothing to do with whether they're good-looking or bad-looking or good actors or not; it's just visceral. I've always said to the actors, "Don't act, please feel it; if it's felt deeply you won't need to act." Because you'll do things that are wonderful, and things that you didn't think of, and things that I would never have dreamt of asking you to do. Like Tom [Hiddleston in *The Deep Blue Sea*] picking up his hat: he goes for it once, twice, three times. And it's because he couldn't get the hat off the wall. But at that moment it's perfect. Who knows, he may have done it subconsciously—it doesn't matter. Also, when you write things, you're not aware of their power. For instance, in *Deep Blue Sea*, he closes the suitcases and clicks it closed. Have you any idea how loud clicks are when people aren't talking? It's deafening. It's wonderful, because I hadn't thought they'd make such a loud noise.

Growing up in a large family, we were all brought up to speak our minds. And it caused a lot of bother sometimes. And afterwards there would be that terrible silence. I do find it almost unbearable. Oh, someone say something, someone do something, just to break the silence! So I'm very aware of silence. And silence is like music. It can be really powerful if used properly in the proper place.

MK: Your films don't follow an A to B to C progression. How important is it to you to tell a narrative in a nonstraightforward way?

TD: What cinema can do is can give you the absolute instantaneous feeling of something that has happened, either in memory or that is happening in the so-called real time. When I was doing *Deep Blue Sea*, I realized that in most of the first act [of the play], Hester is off-stage, and it's Mrs. Elton telling you what happened. It's completely unconvincing. Terence Rattigan never lived in a boarding house in Ladbroke Grove in 1952; he was far too rich. So he has no idea how they talk. And most of the first act is collapsed into nine minutes in the film. And I said to the Rattigan Trust, we've got to go from Hester's point of view. And if it's Hester point of view, anything she's not privy to we can't have. So if you can show it, you don't need someone telling you. But if she's going to kill herself, what would she be thinking of as she went under the gas? She'd be thinking how she got there, why she's doing this. Dead simple. And then you go into those memories, and you come back to her being woken up. And if it's from her point of view, it's more interesting, because you can float in and out of things while she's waiting for him to come home. Of course she'd be thinking about why she did it, how she got there, how she feels about him, when she first met him, when they started to row, when they were in love. I mean, we've all waited for someone to come, and all those things go through our minds. But it's not interesting to say this happened, then this happened, then that happened. When people remember, they remember the intensity of the moment and nothing else. And then you can move in and out of time whenever you like, and make it linear when it should be. I find that much more interesting. Because it's elliptical, it has ambiguity, and if we don't have any ambiguity, then there's no real interest. You can be too ambiguous, too, so you don't know where you are—that's another thing. That's why the films are so difficult to cut. Because if you take one thing out, the effect is huge. That's why the cutting is worrying for me. I always get very, very worried, because they say, "Take that out." Like the two scenes with the mother in *Deep Blue Sea*. I was pressed to take those out. And I said, "No, they've got to be in. I've taken them out in other cuts, and it doesn't work, they've got to be there." And then the audience first saw it, it worked. I said, "I know, that's why I left it in."

MK: So in terms of *The Deep Blue Sea*, it's about being economical. What about with *Distant Voices* and *The Long Day Closes*? At what point did you realize these were not going to be straightforward films?

TD: When I was writing. When my father died, people didn't go to therapy; and if they did, they certainly weren't working-class, and they talked all the time. And I listened to them talking all the time. And their memories sort of became my memories, because I only experienced seven years of my father, which was more than enough. So I got off very lightly. They were wonderful storytellers; I don't think they realized just how good they were. And it was the same with films, when they came and told you what a film was. It was only when I was much older I realized that, of course, they were telling you the story that they *think* they saw, not what was actually there. That's why film is so powerful. And I'd listen all the time to these extraordinary stories, and I just knew that it wasn't something like, "This happened, then that happened, then that happened." It was moving in and out of time. I don't know why I thought that; it was just something that I actually felt. And I just knew it was right. I have absolutely no aesthetic or intellectual argument to sustain it. I just said, "This is what it feels like." I feel all the films. I feel where the shots should be. I feel how it should be told. I don't know why. When I went to the pictures, I could remember entire stretches of dialogue and shots, and I thought everyone could do that. Because nobody told me that they didn't! And I really did believe that what I saw was true. The difference in those days was that most adults were not sophisticated. We thought America was like *Young at Heart*, with these fabulous houses—nobody did any work, they lived wonderfully, they had wraparound teeth, and huge kitchens! There was no poverty; everything was equal. You just believed it. Of course, when I first went to America, I was really disillusioned.

MK: In *Distant Voices, Still Lives*, were Tony, Maisie, and Eileen amalgams of your siblings, or were you sticking to the memories of those three people?

TD: Yes, it was their memories. I couldn't put in many things that happened, because nobody would have believed it. He was so violent. It had to be cut down to essential things. And it was difficult to decide what to leave out. The order of things changed. Certain little details changed for the reasons of the narrative. But basically everything happened, not necessarily in that order. It was a lot worse than what's in the film. I'll give you an example. I'm the youngest. The brother who was closest to me, Kevin, who's dead now, was a babe in arms, and my father went into one of his black silences, and she just said she couldn't take it that day and she picked up Kevin and she ran upstairs, and he ran after her, and she went into the bedroom and jumped out the window. A soldier was walking by and caught her. No one's going to believe that in a movie. When I ran into a room and made a noise, he'd just kick me from one end of the room to the other. And now when I go into a room, and two people have had a row, I can tell [*snaps*] immediately, and I'm all on edge, even though it's got nothing to do with me.

MK: You mentioned before about your discomfort with representations of violence because of your experiences with it. It seems like other than *Distant Voices, The Neon Bible* is the only film that has explicit violence. How did you approach that?

TD: With trepidation, really. And so I said, "Okay, he [Denis Leary's character] has to hit her [Diana Scarwid's character], but it's got to be one blow. I don't want any more than that." It was very difficult, because I saw all the times my Mum was beaten up. It was very, very hard, that. So I didn't look forward to it. They did it very well. And we had a stuntman there to say, "Oh, he looks as though he's not hit her in this or that take." They did it very well, but I was glad when it was over. Because it brought back really horrid memories of being absolutely terrified. People have said *Distant Voices* is violent. I said no, you don't actually see anything, really. It's implied. I think using the song "Taking a Chance on Love" heightens the brutality of it. But it was nothing like as awful as it was.

MK: How did you approach shooting the violent conclusion of *The Neon Bible*?

TD: I just think the violence is not terribly convincing. I don't think I did a particularly good job. I should have been more rigorous with the cutting, I think. That's my fault. It's nobody's fault but mine, and I think that's what makes it weak. But I'm not one for lots of action. And actually, strictly speaking, the way it's shown in that film is true—in real violence there's this dull thud, and they fall over. That's what literally happens. I think the end of the shot works because it's his hand pointing down. And it dissolves to the train. It's like an ogre, like the devil, like conscience. I like that bit. But I don't think it's staged particularly well, because that's an area I'm not that good at. If I did a car chase, it would be two cars going very slowly.

MK: Comedies and musicals are so important and influential to you, but your films are never really either. How have they influenced your work?

TD: Elliptically. I think where I emotionally learned to put music to a moving image is seeing all those musicals. That's where I got my education. You imbibed these things unconsciously. There are bits of comedy in my films, but they're not dominant. I did write a very good comedy script, but couldn't get the money for it. But my overall view of life is not comic. I see the glass as half empty. And as I get older, that has become more intensified. I do like to make people laugh. It's lovely to be made to laugh. But it's very difficult to do it well. And when it's badly done, it's excruciating. When it's wonderfully done, it's a joy. What gave British comedy of the fifties its underlying tension was that the era was very hierarchical, and there were certain ways you couldn't behave. So that if you behaved in a slightly different way it was looked upon as not the right thing to do.

The way it worked in this country was, you'd go to the movies, and you'd have the big picture, usually American, and there was a B picture, and that could be British. But when the British film was a comedy, it was always the big picture. Because we had wonderful people: Alastair Sim, Margaret Rutherford, Joyce Grenfell. Those people were intrinsically funny. We don't have those people anymore. Like we don't have the right people to play Dickens anymore. They've all gone. We had Francis L. Sullivan, who plays Mr. Jaggers and Martita Hunt as Miss Havisham in *Great Expectations* [1947]. Incomparable. These people just can't be bettered. We haven't got them now. And everyone is coerced into making films with feel-good endings. A friend of Edith Wharton did a version of *The House of Mirth* for the theater, and it failed. She asked why it failed; he said, "You don't understand, Edith. Americans want tragedy with a happy ending." It's a contradiction in terms.

MK: Speaking of *The House of Mirth* and tragic endings, I was curious about the "1905 to 1907" bookends, which appear onscreen. You said somewhere you had fought for them. I think it's incredibly powerful, but hard to describe why. Could you explain why you added those years onscreen?

TD: Because I wanted to show that in two years you could destroy someone. In a mere two years. That little short time, and she's destroyed—and helps to destroy herself, one must add. It's not a happy ending, but she comes to know a kind of morality. And she finds integrity at the end. It's cold comfort, because she accidentally kills herself. Although in the film it looks as though she's done it deliberately. And you can't get away from that, unless someone says, "She did it accidentally," which I didn't want. But she reaches an emotional, intellectual, and moral integrity. And that is what helps also to destroy her. But it's a tragic ending as in the book. This is what it's like, this is what society does. And to a certain extent, the savagery of that belle époque society is alive and well in Hollywood. It's exactly the same. You hear stories, and you think, God, how can grown people think this is serious? There was one restaurant. Everyone went there, and the closer you were to the kitchen, the more important you were. And the more important you were, even before you paid the bill your car was valeted. Also in Los Angeles, we did interviews at the Chateau Marmont. You eat outside in the garden, and when people come out to garden, they all go like this [*head turns*], and think "Not important!" and they carry on eating. And when someone who *is* important comes in, you can see them *vibrate* with envy. And you think, how can you live like this? This is so unhealthy and unpleasant. I couldn't survive there for more than a week. In the stairwell as you go inside, there's this faux Caravaggio painting. This woman in the clouds with a voluminous blue dress, looking up, and you can see her thinking, "When will I get a television series?" It's got nothing to do with the real world.

 MK: You're always trying new things. With *Of Time and the City* it was digital video. How did you feel using those different cameras?

 TD: Well, a lot of it was found footage, what was already there. And the little bits and things we did with the digital camera were fine! And in fact, sometimes I wasn't even there. I'd say, "Just go and shoot something." I was there for the shots around St. George's Hall. It's the largest Greco-Roman neoclassical building in Europe, and it's fabulous inside. I said, "Just go and film something," and it sort of emerged that there were lots of shots of little children. And I thought, Well, that should be the motif there. The little children will inherit the world. Eventually they will grow up and replace us. But there was a great sense of freedom, because a lot of the footage wasn't mine, and I was writing the commentary while we were doing it. The trouble was, as always, the people who put up the money; you've got to convince them this or that was right. And that I do find really tiresome. It should be obvious that the sequence goes together. And sometimes you get no response at all. And that's really dispiriting. And my two producers would look at me, I'd look at them, and think this is really hard-going. I never have final cut. I've got to persuade and cajole and hope they'll go along with me. We only had 230,000 pounds to do it, and the average documentary costs 300,000. We had to clear music and archive materials as well. The two people who were clearing it got wonderful deals for us.

MK: Music clearance must always be an issue, because before you shoot you have songs in your head. Does music come before image to you?

TD: It's a mixture. Sometimes the music comes first, sometimes it comes after, sometimes it comes during. I know when it needs music. Like the opening of *Distant Voices, Still Lives*, I knew something was wrong. And I'm a great lover of Radio 3, which is the classical station here on BBC, and I was listening to a concert, and it finished early. And so they always play something as filler till the one o' clock news. And it was Jessye Norman singing "There's a Man Going round Taking Names," and I thought, That's it [*snaps*]. That's what I've been waiting for. And you sort of antenna out. And remembering things you heard *once* forty years ago. God knows where it comes from, and I'm very glad it does come.

When I met Sol [Papadopoulos] and Roy [Boulter] about doing *Of Time and the City,* they asked me if I would be interested in doing a drama. I said no, I've done my Liverpool stuff. They said, how about a documentary, sort of an essay. I said yes, that might be good, I'll have a think about it. Later, as I was driving with [his assistant] John, I thought, Oh God, what have I let myself in for? And I was going to stop the car, ring Sol, and say I'm pulling out, give it to someone else. And we stopped at the lights. And in the late fifties, a lot of slums were pulled down like ours were, in the north, and these new estates built, which in ten years were slums themselves. And I suddenly thought if I had that and Peggy Lee singing "The Folks Who Live on the Hill," then we've got a sequence. And I told them I'll do it. But the song wasn't cleared. And all the way through it wasn't cleared, it wasn't cleared, it wasn't cleared. So I wrote to Peggy Lee's estate. And we didn't hear. And then finally they said yes. Oh, I was *so* relieved! And then we showed the cut to Don Boyd, who said, "You're using a bit of *Four Quartets*," and he had tried to use *The Four Quartets,* and they wouldn't allow it. Eliot did not like cinema. He thought it was vulgar. So I wrote to them. Again, we waited and waited. The very last day, the *very* last day, they said yes.

MK: When did you find the inspiration for Doris Day's "It All Depends on You" for the mother's funeral scene at the beginning of *Death and Transfiguration*? That is the start of that sort of music-and-image juxtaposition in your films.

TD: I love Doris Day doing that song in *Love Me or Leave Me* [1955]. It's just her and a piano. And I remember being taken to see it and just crying like anything. I was eleven. Although the first thing I saw her in was *Young at Heart* [1954]; that's when I first fell in love with her. It's so pure. And I just thought that over these opening sequences it will be right. And I was still getting money from the BFI then, and I said, "So you think we could possibly afford to clear it?" And it cost three thousand pounds, which was a lot of money. And they said, "We'll clear it for you." I thought they would say no. It's such a wonderful song. And, of course, its subtextual implication for the character is that it *does* all depend on his mother. Like it did with me and my mother. My mother was the love of my life. It was very hard when she died, and I loved her with all my heart. I didn't want her to die, although she lived to be ninety and she had a good life after my father died in 1953.

The very first thing we shot it *Death and Transfiguration*, though, was Wilfrid [Brambell] dying on the bed. He was noted in this country as a comedy actor. He was seventy-six. And I said, "I don't want anyone to speak during shooting." We did the first take, and we were all very moved. And this little voice from the bed says, "The Duchess of Bewd in Lahore / Said darling this is such a bore / I'm covered in sweat, you haven't come yet / And look, it's a quarter to four." And these doggerels went on and on, and they got filthier and filthier. It really was a wonderful thing for him to have done. And the other one I remember: "There was a young lady called Alice / who pissed in the Vatican palace / It was not dire need which provoked this foul deed / but sheer Presbyterian malice." He was wonderful. It was a perfect antidote. He was a lovely man. Drank gin virtually raw. He died of cirrhosis. But it was perfect for someone to do that. I thought, My God, you really are a trouper.

MK: What about the actor Terry O'Sullivan, who played the middle-aged Tucker? How was working with him?

TD: Because I could only pay ten pounds a day, I couldn't go to any of the big agencies. So I went to a small agency, and a lot of people were coming in: lads of twenty-four, saying that with makeup they could look forty. I went in for about three days, and on the last day, one man came in who was the right age and said, "I wouldn't do this because it's so sordid." I thought, Okay, I'll see the next person, and then I'll go home.

And Terry came in, and I thought he had such a fabulous face. He said he'd do it. He was tricky to be with, because his was a life not fulfilled. There's nothing you can do about that. And he was difficult about *Death and Transfiguration*, because he said he wasn't available, and I said, "If you can't do it, then I just can't shoot the film." And I said, "You did say you'd keep your word," and he finally said, "Yes, I'll honor it." But you could tell he didn't want to. That hurt me. Because I thought we were friends. But he was a sad man. It was a life unfulfilled, I think, in many areas. And that gives him an extraordinary quality. It's a tragic face. Utterly tragic. But what can you do. I tried to befriend him. I tried to ask him to lunch or go window-shopping, which doesn't cost anything. He said "No, I don't want to do it." So in the end I thought I can't make it better, because I can't do anything about your life any more than anyone can do anything about my life.

MK: How was it casting for your siblings and friends in *Distant Voices, Still Lives* and *The Long Day Closes*? Are you actually looking for people who remind you of them, or is it all about the character in the moment?

TD: It's all about the character and whether they can capture the spirit of who they are playing. Like casting for Monica in *Distant Voices, Still Lives*—she was terrific, that girl. Monica was really like that. We loved when Monica came around. She was just fun. She was a real love, and she was the only person who could get around my father. She could always charm him. We were showing *Long Day Closes* in Liverpool, and I hadn't spoken to Monica in years. Hadn't physically seen her, so I didn't know what she looked like. I'd sent an invitation out, and of course no one replies, so I thought, She must have moved. I did have her address. Anyway, I did the Q&A, and I walked up the steps, and this woman stops me and says, "Hiya, Bud." Because I was called Bud at home. Oh, it was fifty-odd years, it was wonderful to see her. And she told me a terrible story that really broke my heart. She came around one day to go out with Eileen, and my mother, at the door, said to her quietly, "Will you comb my hair? He won't let me comb my hair." And I thought, You bastard! Not to let her comb her hair. She said she quickly combed it. It's unimaginable. He wouldn't let her go out.

MK: So after your father died, how fast was it for your mother to emerge from this shell and in a sense rejoin the world?

TD: Getting your hair done was expensive, and the first thing my three sisters did was they clubbed together and got her hair done. And she came home, and I thought she looked so beautiful. And that was when she started to live. For a couple of weeks afterwards, she'd go out to shop, and she'd say, "I've got to go home, Tommy's there." And my sisters would say, "You don't have to go, he's dead now, you can do what you like." And she then began to live and have a happy time—and live to be ninety, I'm glad to say.

After he died, our house became a magnet. Everyone came. Fridays were fabulous, because all my sisters' girlfriends came, and I was allowed to buy their makeup. It was just fabulous. Loved Fridays. I can *smell* them even now. That house was wonderful. The atmosphere was rich, and the street was so vibrant. It was a real community. I loved that house. That's where my spiritual home is. Fridays were utterly fabulous. We used to get Pancake makeup and Majestic Red lipstick, and nylons, American type, no seam, because seams were considered tarty. And I'd get most of that from the chemist's. And they had these "color boys." I don't know if you ever had them in America. They were these huge glasses filled with colored water. I loved going there. It was lit by gas, all green interior. We had nothing. But we had each other. Every Christmas, she would borrow twenty-five pounds from a lending company, and you had to pay what was the equivalent of twenty-six pounds fifty back. And that was a lot of money. She got everything for those twenty-five pounds for Christmas. She was terrified of missing a payment, because they wouldn't renew the loan next year. She made Christmas wonderful. I hate Christmas now. It's also her birthday on the twenty-third, so I miss her doubly. Those days and Mother's Day are very hard. I go everywhere and see all those Mother's Day cards and I think, I can't send her one now. But I told her I love her every day, just in case.

MK: Do you see your siblings at the holidays?

TD: Well, they're starting to die, I'm afraid. Two brothers are dead; three sisters are alive. But everyone lives in Liverpool. They wouldn't all come down here. So I don't go up that often, because Liverpool is full of memories. Everywhere I look there's memories. And everything I knew has been pulled down, changed into a shopping mall or something. I look around and think this is not the place I grew up in and loved. And I've changed. I've been lucky. I've gone all over the world, which is nice. But

I couldn't go back to live there, I just couldn't. Anyway, I've found my little home here, and I'm happy here. It's not the same as 18 Kensington Street, nothing ever will be. But I've got good neighbors, and I've got good friends. It's pretty. So I really shouldn't grumble. But I'm going to!

MK: When you're making movies and you're re-creating things from when you're a child, are you so invested in the minutiae of the shot that it's easy to get away from the past, or are you actually sensing the experience of the past while you're making it?

TD: I'm not experiencing the past; I know when it's got to be accurate. I remember not just what the fifties looked like, I remember what it *felt* like, and that's a different thing. The usual mistake is when a film is set in 1953 everything looks like it was *made* in 1953. It wasn't like that. The credit restrictions weren't eased till the sixties, so lots of people had stuff that went back to Edwardian times, because that's what they had all their lives. My father's mother, who lived two doors up, had this huge ebony wardrobe, I don't know how on earth they got it up into this tiny house. I know about those sorts of details, because I just remember them. Like, for instance, smoking. Cigarettes weren't tipped. So when you took your first drag, you always went like this [*mimes taking tobacco off the tip of his tongue with his thumb and forefinger*]. I thought it looked terribly sophisticated. I've never smoked, but I love the way they handled them, the paraphernalia of smoking. I was in a play in drama school in which I was pretending to smoke. It looks pathetic! Hopeless.

MK: And you feel the same way about fiction films, based on other people's material? They all have this sense of rich experience.

TD: As soon as I read *The House of Mirth*, I knew what the opening shots were. I just knew. Then I can do it. It's the same with *The Deep Blue Sea*. To a lesser extent, because I had to read it a few times before I knew what the subtextual meaning was, because the surface story is unremarkable. But when I knew it was about love, I thought, I know how to do it now. And it's got to be from Hester's point of view. And it's got to be true. And things influence you subliminally. When my sisters started to get married, they went into these rooms. I can't tell you how awful they were. My sister Eileen got married and went into this one room above a pawnshop. Each place was just one room. And it was all this old furniture. And really old twenties furniture has dark mahogany, and it's got that cheap gray marble, which I detest. I used to hate going there. I loathed that room. For *The Deep Blue Sea*, I said it's got to have that look about it. Everything's faded, everything's old, everything's shabby. Britain was shabby. It's really difficult to explain to someone, but James Merifield, our wonderful production designer, got it right away. And Florian Hoffmeister is wonderful, one of the great cinematographers, I think. To Ruth Myers, who did all the costumes, I said, "Please, it's got to look like they've all been wearing these clothes, not like they just stepped out of wardrobe." And she did; they just look right. This is what I found truly thrilling: she said about Hester that when she left her husband she took one good coat, and it's claret. That coat looks so rich. You didn't see primary color much back then. And it's ravishing; *she's* ravishing. They're artists in their own right. I find that incredibly thrilling. I wouldn't have thought of that.

MK: For your next film, *Sunset Song*, do you have your crew?

TD: I'm going to get as many of the crew as we had on *Deep Blue Sea* as possible. They were a fabulous crew. I want to work with them forever and ever and ever. Yes, I absolutely want them. They know we have to go into preproduction this year. We will know sometime this month whether we get the final bit of money. But it's all cast. Agyness Deyn plays the main role, and Peter Mullan is playing her father. The other actors are not well known. She's going to be marvelous, that girl. I'd never heard of her, but apparently she's a model. She came in and looked about eleven years old. And she was the very first person and it was the best performance. And the other girls who came in weren't right, but some of them would be good in supporting parts. Peter Mullan came all the way down from Scotland; I quite wrongly thought he lived in London. I said, "You haven't come all the way down from Scotland, have you? I would have given it to you over the phone!" He has a wonderful sense of humor. Very funny. A lovely man. So hopefully we start preproduction this year.

MK: You've wanted to make this for a long time.

TD: Over ten years. It's set before, during, and after the First World War, about these subsistence farmers in Scotland.

MK: And do you have the whole movie mapped out already, as you normally do?

TD: Yes! Talk about anally retentive. One day, I'll do a storyboard, I promise!

Filmography

Children (1976)
United Kingdom
Production: British Film Institute
Producer: Peter Shannon
Director: Terence Davies
Screenplay: Terence Davies
Cinematographer: William Diver
Assistant Director: Dave Wheeler
Editors: Digby Rumsey and Sarah Ellis
Sound Recordist: Digby Rumsey
Executive Production Supervisor: Geoffrey Evans
Cast: Phillip Mawdsley (Tucker as a boy), Nick Stringer (Father), Val Lilley (Mother), Robin Hooper (Tucker at 24), Colin Hignett (Bully), Robin Bowen (Bully), Harry Wright (Teacher), Phillip Joseph (Teacher), Trevor Eve (Man in shower), Linda Beckett (Neighbor)
16mm, black-and-white
43 min.

Madonna and Child (1980)
United Kingdom
Production: National Film School
Producer: Mike Maloney
Director: Terence Davies
Screenplay: Terence Davies
Cinematographer: William Diver
Assistant Cinematographer: Sergio Leon
Editor: Mick Audsley
Sound Recordist: Antoinette de Bromhead
Cast: Terry O'Sullivan (Tucker), Sheila Raynor (Mother), Paul Barber (Tattooist), John Meynell (Priest), Brian Ward (Man in club), Dave Cooper (Tattooed man), Mark Walton (Second man)

16mm, black-and-white
30 min.

Death and Transfiguration (1983)
United Kingdom
Production: The Greater London Arts Association and the British Film Institute
Producer: Claire Barwell
Director: Terence Davies
Screenplay: Terence Davies
Cinematographer: William Diver
Editor: Mick Audsley
Art Director: Miki van Zwanenberg
Sound: Mohammed Hassini, Charles Patey, and Mark Frith
Cast: Wilfrid Brambell (Tucker as an old man), Terry O'Sullivan (Tucker, middle-aged), Iain Munro (Tucker at 11), Jeanne Doree (Mother), Chrissy Roberts (Nurse), Virginia Donovan (Nurse), Carol Christmas (Nun)
16mm, black-and-white
23 min.

Distant Voices, Still Lives (1988)
United Kingdom
Production: British Film Institute, in association with Film Four International
Distribution: Avenue Entertainment
Producer: Jennifer Howarth
Director: Terence Davies
Screenplay: Terence Davies
Executive Producer: Colin MacCabe
Cinematographers: William Diver and Patrick Duval
Editor: William Diver
Art Directors: Miki van Zwanenberg and Jocelyn James
Costume Designer: Monica Howe
Cast: Freda Dowie (Mother), Pete Postlethwaite (Father), Angela Walsh (Eileen), Dean Williams (Tony), Lorraine Ashbourne (Maisie), Michael Starke (Dave), Vincent Maguire (George), Antonia Mallen (Rose), Debi Jones (Micky), Chris Darwin (Red), Marie Jelliman (Jingles), Andrew Schofield (Les), Anny Dyson (Granny)
35mm, color
85 min.

The Long Day Closes (1992)
United Kingdom
Production: British Film Institute and Film Four International
Distribution: Sony Pictures Classics

Producer: Olivia Stewart
Director: Terence Davies
Screenplay: Terence Davies
Executive Producers: Ben Gibson and Colin MacCabe
Director of Photography: Michael Coulter
Editor: William Diver
Production Designer: Christopher Hobbs
Art Director: Kate Naylor
Costume Designer: Monica Howe
Music Supervisor: Bob Last
Music Director: Robert Lockhart
Executive in Charge of Production: Angela Topping
Cast: Leigh McCormack (Bud), Marjorie Yates (Mother), Anthony Watson (Kevin), Nicholas Lamont (John), Ayse Owens (Helen), Tina Malone (Edna), Jimmy Wilde (Curly), Robin Polley (Mr. Nicholls), Peter Ivatts (Mr. Bushell), Kirk McLaughlin (Laborer/Christ), Brenda Peters (Nurse), Karl Skeggs (Albie)
35mm, color
85 min.

The Neon Bible (1995)
United States
Production: Channel Four Films/Scala
Distribution: Strand Releasing
Producers: Elizabeth Karlsen and Olivia Stewart
Director: Terence Davies
Screenplay: Terence Davies
Based on the Novel by: John Kennedy Toole
Director of Photography: Michael Coulter
Production Designer: Christopher Hobbs
Editor: Charles Rees
Costume Designer: Monica Howe
Music Director: Robert Lockhart
Cast: Gena Rowlands (Aunt Mae), Jacob Tierney (David aged 15), Drake Bell (David aged 10), Diana Scarwid (Sarah), Denis Leary (Frank), Leo Burmester (Bobbie Lee Taylor), Frances Conroy (Miss Scover), Peter McRobbie (Reverend Williams)
35mm, color
91 min.

The House of Mirth (2000)
United Kingdom
Production: Granada Film Limited

Producer: Olivia Stewart
Director: Terence Davies
Screenplay: Terence Davies
Based on the Novel by: Edith Wharton
Cinematographer: Remi Adefarasin
Editor: Michael Parker
Production Designer: Don Taylor
Art Director: Kate Naylor
Costume Designer: Monica Howe
Music Director: Adrian Johnston
Cast: Gillian Anderson (Lily Bart), Eric Stoltz (Lawrence Selden), Anthony LaPaglia (Sim Rosedale), Eleanor Bron (Mrs. Peniston), Laura Linney (Bertha Dorset), Dan Akyroyd (Gus Trenor), Terry Kinney (George Dorset), Jodhi May (Grace Stepney), Elizabeth McGovern (Carry Fisher), Penny Downie (Judy Trenor), Pearce Quigley (Percy Gryce)
35mm, color
140 min.

Of Time and the City (2008)
United Kingdom
Production: Northwest Vision and Media, Digital Departures, and Hurricane Films
Distribution: Strand Releasing
Producers: Sal Papadopoulos and Ray Boulter
Director: Terence Davies
Screenplay: Terence Davies
Director of Photography: Tim Pollard
Editor: Liza Ryan-Carter
Archive Producer: Jim Anderson
Music Supervisor: Ian Neil
Narrator: Terence Davies
Digital video and mixed archival film footage, color/black and white
74 min.

The Deep Blue Sea (2011)
United Kingdom
Production: U.K. Film Council and Film Four
Producers: Sean O'Connor and Kate Ogborn
Director: Terence Davies
Screenplay: Terence Davies
Based on the Play by: Terence Rattigan
Director of Photography: Florian Hoffmeister
Editor: David Charap

Production Designer: James Merifield
Costume Designer: Ruth Myers
Music Supervisor: Ian Neil
Cast: Rachel Weisz (Hester Collyer), Tom Hiddleston (Freddie Page), Simon Russell Beale (Sir William Collyer), Ann Mitchell (Mrs. Elton), Barbara Jefford (Collyer's mother), Nicolas Amer (Mr. Elton), Jolyon Coy (Philip Welch), Karl Johnson (Mr. Miller)
35mm, color
98 min.

Bibliography

Abbott, Kate. "How We Made: Terence Davies and Freda Dowie on *Distant Voices, Still Lives.*" *The Guardian*, April 16, 2012. Accessed December 28, 2013. http://www.guardian.co.uk/film/2012/apr/16/how-we-made-distant-voices-still-lives.

Altman, Rick. *The American Film Musical*. Bloomington: Indiana University Press, 1987.

Anderson, Jason. "My Liverpool: Terence Davies' *Of Time and the City.*" *Cinema Scope* 35 (Summer 2008). Accessed December 28, 2013. http://cinema-scope.com/cinema-scope-magazine/interviews-features-my-liverpool-terence-davies'-of-time-and-the-city/.

Anderson, Lindsay. "Only Connect: Some Aspects of the Work of Humphrey Jennings." In *The British Avant-Garde Film, 1926–1995: An Anthology of Writings*. Ed. Michael O'Pray. London: University of Luton Press, 1996. 87–96. (First published in *Sight and Sound*, April–June 1954.)

Andrew, Geoff. "Reckless Moment." *Sight and Sound* 21.12 (December 2011): 18–24.

Antonini, Agnese. *Vermeer: The Complete Works*. Trans. Lawrence Jenkens. New York: Barnes and Noble, 2007. Originally published by Rusconi Library, 2004.

Bainbridge, Beryl. "Bittersweet Symphony." *The Guardian*, April 20, 2007.

Barker, Adam. Rev. of *Distant Voices, Still Lives*. *Monthly Film Bulletin* 55.657 (October 1988). (Reprinted in booklet for DVD edition of *Distant Voices, Still Lives* [London: British Film Institute, 2005].)

Barr, Charles. *All Our Yesterdays: 90 Years of British Cinema*. London: British Film Institute, 1986.

Barrie, David. "The Dirty Truth." *The Guardian*, August 18, 2002.

Bazin, André. "The Ontology of the Photographic Image." In *What Is Cinema? Volume 1*. Trans. Hugh Gray. Berkeley: University of California Press, 1967. 9–16.

Bibbiani, William. "There Are Sharks: An Interview with Terence Davies." Crave Online, March 21, 2012. Accessed December 28, 2013. http://www

.craveonline.com/film/articles/185233-there-are-sharks-an-interview-with-terence-davies.

Cahir, Linda Costanzo. "The House of Mirth: An Interview with Director Terence Davies and Producer Olivia Stewart." *Literature/Film Quarterly* 29.3 (2001): 166–71.

Cairns, David. "Right City, Wrong Time." *Shadowplay* blog, June 30, 2008. Accessed December 28, 2013. http://dcairns.wordpress.com/2008/06/30/right-city-wrong-time/.

Caughie, John. "Half Way to Paradise." *Sight and Sound* 2.1 (May 1992): 11–13.

Christensen, Claus. "A Vast Edifice of Memories: The Cyclical Cinema of Terence Davies." *POV: A Danish Journal of Film Studies* 6 (December 1998): 125–39.

Clarke, Donald. "Being Gay Has Ruined My Life" (Interview with Terence Davies). *Irish Times*, November 25, 2011. http://www.irishtimes.com/newspaper/theticket/2011/1125/1224308080967.html.

Coe, Jonathan. "Jolly and Grim." *Sight and Sound* 5.10 (October 1995): 12–14.

Concannon, Philip. "An Interview with Terence Davies." Phil on Film, October 24, 2008. Accessed December 28, 2013. http://www.philonfilm.net/2008/10/interview-terence-davies.html.

Corless, Kieron. "Formula Free: Kieron Corless Talks to Co-producer Solon Papadopoulos." *Sight and Sound* 18.11 (November 2008): 47.

———. "Listen to Liverpool" (Interview with Terence Davies). *Sight and Sound* 18.6 (June 2008): 22.

Corrigan, Timothy. *The Essay Film*. New York: Oxford University Press, 2011.

Costello, Ray. *Black Liverpool: The Early History of Britain's Oldest Black Community, 1730–1918*. Birkenhead, U.K.: Birkenhead Press, 2001.

Danks, Adrian. "The Art of Memory: Terence Davies' *Distant Voices, Still Lives*." *Metro* 116 (1998): 53–54.

Davies, Terence. "Four Songs at Twilight." *The Guardian*, October 12, 2001. Accessed December 28, 2013. http://www.guardian.co.uk/books/2001/oct/13/books.guardianreview1.

———. "The Greatest Films Poll." *Sight and Sound* 22.9 (September 2012): 63.

———. *Hallelujah Now*. London: Penguin Books, 1984.

———. *A Modest Pageant*. London: Faber and Faber, 1992.

Davis, Nick. *The Desiring-Image: Gilles Deleuze and Contemporary Queer Cinema*. New York: Oxford University Press, 2013.

Deleuze, Gilles. *Cinema 2: The Time-Image*. Minneapolis: University of Minnesota Press, 1989. (First published as *Cinéma 2, L'image-temps* [Paris: Les editions de minuets, 1985].)

Dixon, Wheeler Winston. *Collected Interviews: Voices from Twentieth-Century Cinema*. Carbondale: Southern Illinois University Press, 2001.

Durgnat, Raymond. "Two Social Problem Films: *Sapphire* and *Victim*." In *Liberal Directions: Basil Dearden and Postwar British Film Culture*. Ed. Alan

Burton, Tim O'Sullivan, and Paul Wells. Wiltshire, U.K.: Flicks Books, 1997. 59–88.

Dyer, Richard. *Brief Encounter.* London: British Film Institute, 1993.

Ehrenstein, David. "A Director's Struggle with Art and His Beginnings." *Los Angeles Times,* July 2, 1993.

Eliot, T. S. *The Four Quartets.* San Diego: Harcourt, Brace, and Co., 1943.

Ellis, Jim. "Temporality and Queer Consciousness in *The House of Mirth.*" *Screen* 47.2 (Summer 2006): 163–78.

———. "Terence Davies and the *Unheimlich* Home Movie." In *British Queer Cinema.* Ed. Robin Griffiths. London: Routledge. 133–44.

Everett, Wendy. *Terence Davies.* Manchester: Manchester University Press, 2004.

Fairbrother, Trevor. *John Singer Sargent: The Sensualist.* Seattle: Seattle Art Museum, 2000.

Farley, Paul. *BFI Modern Classics: Distant Voices Still Lives.* London: British Film Institute, 2006.

Feeney, Mark. "Terence Davies Discusses Presence of Past in His Films." *Boston Globe,* March 24, 2012. Accessed January 16, 2014. http://www.boston.com/2012/03/24/davies/WcdrAqK77eWnQ13HrTKQMM/singlepage.html.

Feuer, Jane. *The Hollywood Musical.* Bloomington: Indiana University Press, 1993.

Francke, Lizzie. "From the Inside Out." *Sight and Sound* 5.10 (October 1995): 16–17.

Freud, Sigmund. "Screen Memories." In *The Uncanny.* Trans. David McLintock. London: Penguin Classics, 2003. 1–22.

Freeman, Elizabeth. *Time Binds: Queer Temporalities, Queer Histories.* Durham, N.C,: Duke University Press, 2010.

Fuller, Graham. "Love among the Ruins." *Film Comment* 48.2 (March–April 2012): 40–45.

———. "Summer's End." *Film Comment* 27.1 (January–February 2001): 54–59.

Gilbey, Ryan. "The Mersey Sound." *Sight and Sound* 18.11 (November 2008): 46–47.

Grierson, John. "The Documentary Producer." *Cinema Quarterly* 2.1 (Autumn 1933): 7–9.

Guthmann, Edward. Rev. of *The Neon Bible. San Francisco Chronicle,* July 10, 1996.

Hammond, Wally. "Terence Davies: Interview." *Time Out London* (October 2008). Accessed December 28, 2013. http://www.timeout.com/film/features/show-feature/5872/Terence_Davies-interview.html.

Harrison-Kahan, Lori. "'Queer Myself for Good and All': *The House of Mirth* and the Fictions of Lily's Whiteness." *Legacy* 21.1 (2004): 34–49.

Hattenstone, Simon. "Bigmouth Strikes Again" (Interview with Terence Davies). *The Guardian,* October 19, 2006. Accessed December 28, 2013. http://www.guardian.co.uk/film/2006/oct/20/3.

———. "First Steps in Show Business" (Interview with Terence Davies). *The Guardian*, October 5, 2000. Accessed December 28, 2013. http://www.guardian.co.uk/film/2000/oct/06/culture.features.

Higson, Andrew. "'Britain's Outstanding Contribution to the Film': The Documentary-Realist Tradition." In *All Our Yesterdays: 90 Years of British Cinema*. Ed. Charles Barr. London: British Film Institute, 1986. 72–97.

Hill, John. *Sex, Class, and Realism: British Cinema 1956–1963*. London: British Film Institute, 1986.

Hillis, Aaron. "Interview: Terence Davies on *Of Time and the City*." IFC.com, January 15, 2009. Accessed December 28, 2013. http://www.ifc.com/fix/2009/01/terence-davies-on-of-time-and.

Hoberman, J. "The Inner Light of Terence Davies." *New York Review of Books* NYR Blog, March 23, 2012. Accessed December 28, 2013. http://www.nybooks.com/blogs/nyrblog/2012/mar/23/inner-light-terence-davies/.

———. "The Long Day Closes." In *The Magic Hour: Film at Fin de Siècle*. Philadelphia: Temple University Press, 2003. 41–43. (Originally published as "The Rapture," *Village Voice*, June 1, 1993.)

Hoffmeister, Florian. "Intimate Lighting." *Sight and Sound* 21.12 (December 2011): 20–23.

Horne, Philip. "Beauty's Slow Fade." *Sight and Sound* 10.10 (October 2000): 14–18.

Houston, Penelope. "Cannes 41." *Sight and Sound* 57.3 (Summer 1988): 174–75.

Howarth, Jennifer. "The Child Within." *Sight and Sound* 4.9 (September 1994): 59.

Jack, Ian. "It Was Hailed as a Great Work of Cinema—It Made People Cry." *The Guardian*, October 3, 2008.

Jackson, Kevin. *Humphrey Jennings*. New York: Picador, 2004.

James, Nick. "Two Weeks in Another World." *Sight and Sound* 21.12 (December 2011): 20–24.

Kenny, Moira. "Foundations for the Future." *China Daily—Europe*, November 16, 2012. Accessed December 28, 2013. http://europe.chinadaily.com.cn/epaper/2012–11/16/content_15935826.htm.

Kirk, Russell. *Eliot and His Age*. Wilmington, Del.: Intercollegiate Studies Institute, 2008.

Kirkham, Pat, and Mike O'Shaugnessy. "Designing Desire." *Sight and Sound* 2.1 (May 1992): 13–15.

Lahr, John. *The Diaries of Kenneth Tynan*. New York: Bloomsbury, 2001.

Lees, Andrew. *The Hurricane Port: A Social History of Liverpool*. Edinburgh: Mainstream Publishing, 2011.

Leys, Ruth. *Trauma: A Genealogy*. Chicago: University of Chicago Press, 2000.

Lim, Dennis. "Remembrance of Liverpool Past." *New York Times*, January 9, 2009, AR17.

Love, Heather. *Feeling Backward: Loss and the Politics of Queer History*. Boston: Harvard University Press, 2009.

MacCabe, Colin. *The Eloquence of the Vulgar*. London: British Film Institute, 1999.

Macnab, Geoffrey. "Unseen British Cinema." In *British Cinema of the 90s*. Ed. Robert Murphy. London: British Film Institute, 2000. 135–44.

O'Connor, Sean. "From Stage to Screen: Terence Rattigan, Terence Davies, and *The Deep Blue Sea*." In *The Deep Blue Sea*, by Terence Davies. London: Nick Hearn Books, 2011. iii–viii.

Orr, John. *Cinema and Modernity*. Cambridge: Polity Press, 1993.

Pendreigh, Brian. "An Old-Fashioned Gill." *The Guardian*, June 11, 1999. Accessed December 28, 2013. http://www.guardian.co.uk/film/1999/jun/11/2.

Pinkerton, Nick. "The Power of Restraint in the Films of Terence Davies." *Village Voice*, March 14, 2012. Accessed December 28, 2013. http://www.villagevoice.com/2012-03-14/film/the-power-of-restraint-in-the-films-of-terence-davies/.

Powrie, Phil. "The Family Portrait: Trauma and the *Punctum* in *Distant Voices, Still Lives*." In *Critical Studies—The Seeing Century: Film, Vision, and Identity*. Ed. Wendy Everett. Amsterdam: Editions Rodopi B.V, 2000. 20–35.

Pulleine, Tim. "Still Lives." *Sight and Sound* 57.1 (Winter 1987–88): 4–5.

Quart, Leonard. "Remembering Liverpool: An Interview with Terence Davies." *Cineaste* 34.2 (March 2009). Accessed January 16, 2014. http://www.cineaste.com/articles/remembering-liverpool-an-interview-with-terence-davies.

Ratcliff, Carter. *John Singer Sargent*. New York: Abbeville Press, 2001.

Rattigan, Terence. *The Deep Blue Sea*. London: Nick Hearn Books, 2011.

Rebellato, Dan. "Terence Rattigan: 1911–1977." In *The Deep Blue Sea*, by Terence Davies. London: Nick Hearn Books, 2011. xi–xxv.

Reichert, Jeff. "Outside, Looking In." *Reverse Shot* 24 (June 2009). Accessed December 28, 2013. http://www.reverseshot.com/article/house_mirth.

Rich, B. Ruby. *New Queer Cinema: The Director's Cut*. Durham, N.C.: Duke University Press, 2013.

Roddick, Nick. "The King of Cannes." *London Evening Standard*, May 23, 2008. Accessed December 28, 2013. http://www.standard.co.uk/arts/film/the-king-of-cannes-6697460.html.

Romney, Jonathan. Rev. of *The Deep Blue Sea*. *Sight and Sound* 21.12 (December 2011): 57–58.

Rosenbaum, Jonathan. "Are You Having Fun?" *Sight and Sound* 59.2 (Spring 1990): 96–100.

———. *Essential Cinema*. Baltimore: Johns Hopkins University Press, 2004.

———. "These Magic Moments." *Chicago Reader*, April 5, 1996. Accessed January 16, 2014. http://www.chicagoreader.com/chicago/these-magic-moments/Content?oid=890155.

Sarris, Andrew. *The American Cinema*. New York: E. P. Dutton and Co., 1968.

Schwartz, David. "A Pinewood Dialogue with Terence Davies" (Transcript). New York: Museum of the Moving Image. December 15, 2000. Accessed December

28, 2013. http://www.movingimagesource.us/files/dialogues/2/62815_programs_transcript_html_221.htm.

Sicinski, Michael. "We Sing, but Not Ourselves: Terence Davies' *The Deep Blue Sea*." *Cinema Scope* Online. Accessed December 28, 2013. http://cinema-scope.com/currency/we-sing-but-not-ourselves-terence-davies-the-deep-blue-sea/.

Stratton, David. Rev. of *The Neon Bible*. *Variety*, May 23, 1995.

Tarkovsky, Andrey. *Sculpting in Time*. Trans. Kitty Hunter-Blair. Austin: University of Texas Press, 1986.

"Ten Facts about Liverpool." *The Telegraph*, June 4, 2003.

Thomson, David. *The New Biographical Dictionary of Film*. New York: Alfred A. Knopf, 2002.

Tinkcom, Matthew. *Working Like a Homosexual: Camp, Capital, Cinema*. Durham, N.C.: Duke University Press, 2002.

Toole, John Kennedy. *The Neon Bible*. New York: Grove Press, 1989.

Turner, Graeme. *British Cultural Studies: An Introduction*. London: Routledge, 1996.

Tynan, Kenneth. "The Voice of the Young." Rev. of *Look Back in Anger*. *The Observer*, May 12, 1956.

Walker, Elsie. "Editorial: A Reflection on Forty Years." *Literature/Film Quarterly* 40.4 (2012). Accessed January 16, 2014. http://www.salisbury.edu/lfq/letter_from_the_ed_40_4.htm.

Walsh, David. "Terence Davies' *The House of Mirth*: A Comment and a Press Conference with the Director." World Socialist Web Site, December 28, 2000. Accessed December 28, 2013. http://www.wsws.org/articles/2000/dec2000/mirt-d28.shtml.

Wharton, Edith. *The House of Mirth*. New York: Signet Classic, 2000.

White, Armond. *The Resistance: Ten Years of Pop Culture That Shook the World*. Woodstock, N.Y.: Overlook Press, 1995.

Williams, Tony. "The Masochistic Fix: Gender Oppression in the Films of Terence Davies." In *Fires Were Started: British Cinema and Thatcherism*. Ed. Lester D. Friedman. Minneapolis: University of Minnesota Press, 1993. 243–56.

Wilson, David. "Family Album: *Distant Voices, Still Lives*." *Sight and Sound* 57.4 (Autumn 1988): 282–83.

Woodward, Adam. Terence Davies interview. *Little White Lies* online, November 25, 2011. Accessed December 28, 2013. http://www.littlewhitelies.co.uk/features/articles/terence-davies-17170.

Index

Adefarasin, Remi, 83
Akerman, Chantal, 98
Ali: Fear Eats the Soul (1974), 55
All That Heaven Allows (1955), 55, 129
Anderson, Gillian, 52, 55, 81–82, 86
Anderson, Lindsay, 91
Anger, Kenneth, 10, 47, 100
"Angry Young Man" genre, 91, 93–94
Antonioni, Michelangelo, 115
Arlen, Harold, 66
Avalon (1990), 13

Bacarisse, Salvador, 75
"Barbara Allen" (song), 66
Barber, Samuel, 75
Bazin, André, 113, 121
BBC Radio, 123n7
Beatles, The, 97, 99
Benton, Thomas Hart, 80–81
Berlin, Irving, 66
Billy Liar (1962), 92
black-and-white cinematography, 30, 76, 129–30
bleach-bypass printing process, 77, 130–31
"Blow the Wind Southerly" (song), 78
Boccherini, Luigi, 120
Bogarde, Dirk, 46
Brambell, Wilfrid, 51, 123n3, 142
Branesti, Popescu, 75
Brief Encounter (1945), 57, 91, 93, 103
British comedy, 138–39
British film industry, 16
British Film Institute Production Board, 16, 27, 62, 130, 142

British New Wave, 91–94
British realism, 12, 90–94, 134–35
Britten, Benjamin, 117
Browning Version, The (1948 play), 94
Browning Version, The (1951 film), 94
Bruckner, Anton, 126, 128

camera techniques: crane shot in *The Deep Blue Sea*, 4; crane shot in *Distant Voices, Still Lives*, 100–101; crane shots in *The Long Day Closes*, 36, 71, 104; crane shot in *The Neon Bible*, 35–36; crane shot in *Of Time and the City*, 24; long take in *Children*, 98; long take in *The Deep Blue Sea*, 58–59; long take in *The Long Day Closes* 85–89; pan in *The Long Day Closes*, 87–88; shot planning, 62–63; tracking shot in *Distant Voices, Still Lives*, 112; tracking shots in *The Long Day Closes*, 32, 72–74; tracking shot in *Madonna and Child*, 49; tracking shots in *The Neon Bible*, 41, 74; zoom in *Children*, 2–4, 132–33
Cannes Film Festival, 34
Carmichael, Hoagy, 66
Carousel (1956), 105
Channel 4, 28
Children (1976): autobiographical elements in, 39, 50; homosexual desire in, 42–45; morbidity of, 64; preproduction, 27; principal cast and crew of, 147; sadomasochism in, 47–48; school bullying in, 30–31; use of long take, 98; use of zoom lens, 2–4, 132–33

Chorley, Henry, 122–23
Cinema Now (BBC radio show), 129
Citizen Kane (1941), 110
Cole, Nat King, 99, 104
color in Davies's films, 76–79, 130
conservatism of Davies's cinema, 89–106
Coulter, Michael, 78
Coventry Drama School, 27, 129
Coward, Noël, 55
Crying Game, The (1992), 10

Davies, Terence: Catholicism, 25, 26–27, 128, 131; celibacy, 9, 82, 131; childhood, 25–26, 29–30; childhood and abuse, 25, 127, 137–38; childhood and movie love, 26, 45–46, 91, 100, 128–29; childhood and nostalgia, 95–96; childhood and stasis, 122; childhood and unreliability of memories, 136–37; father, 38, 112; father's death, 39, 136, 143–44; homosexuality and religion, 26, 33; homosexuality and sadomasochism, 46–47; homosexuality and shame 1, 26, 33, 42–43, 45–47, 95–96, 131; mother 142–44; religion and guilt, 50; religion and trauma, 33, 131; rejection of Catholicism, 26–27, 128, 131; siblings, 76–77, 131, 137, 144; teenage years 26–27, 45–46, 50, 92
Day, Doris, 65–66, 141–42
Dearden, Basil, 45–46
Death and Transfiguration (1983): climax of, 51–52; homosexual desire in, 43, 47, 49; opening scene, 64–66; principal cast and crew of, 148; production, 27; sadomasochism in, 49; use of music, 64–66, 141–42
Death in Venice (1971), 132
Death of Nelson, The (painting), 133
Deep Blue Sea, The (2011): as adaptation, 15, 56, 59; autobiographical elements in, 58–59; and *Brief Encounter*, 57–58; closing scene, 1–4; empty spaces in, 115; eroticism in, 56–57; Hester as queer figure, 43, 52, 56–60; lighting, 80; music in, 69–70, 75–76; nonlinearity of, 56, 116, 135–36; opening sequence, 56, 75–76; origins of production, 15–16; painterly qualities, 80; patience of filming actors, 134–35; principal cast and crew of, 150–51; set design and costumes, 145–46; time in, 115–16, 119–20
Deep Blue Sea, The (play), 56, 94, 135
Deleuze, Gilles, 5, 27, 109, 112–17
Deyn, Agyness, 146
Dickinson, Emily, 128
Digital Departures, 15
directing actors, 133
Distant Voices, Still Lives (1988): aesthetic qualities of, 12–13, 76–77, 111–12, 114–15, 130–31; autobiographical elements in, 29, 37–41, 137; camera perspective in, 114–15; casting of, 143; color in, 76–77, 130–31; empty spaces in, 114–15; Liverpool in, 22; memory and, 104–5, 110; movie references in, 100–102; music in, 40, 67–68, 70, 141; nonlinearity of, 29; opening scene, 114–15; photographic tableaux, 111–12; politics of, 89–90; production of, 28, 62; principal cast and crew of, 148; time and, 108–9; 116–18; violence in, 137–38; World War II as depicted in, 58
Diver, William, 76
documentary filmmaking, 15–16, 18–25, 90–91, 93
Douglas, Bill, 97

Ealing Studios, 91
Eliot, T. S. See *Four Quartets*
England: class inequality in, 92–94; homophobia of 1950s, 45, 89, 95–96, 131; pop culture in 1960s, 97; postwar economic boom, 92–93; social landscape of 1950s, 92–94, 96–97; working class in, 96–97; youth culture in, 93–94, 97
Every Day Except Christmas (1957), 91

Fain, Sammy, 66, 100
Family, The (1987), 13
Family Favourites (BBC radio show), 69
Far from Heaven (2002), 55
Fassbinder, Rainer Werner, 55

160 | Index

Ferrier, Kathleen, 78
Fires Were Started (1943), 23
Fitzgerald, Ella, 40
Flaherty, Robert, 24
"Folks Who Live on the Hill, The" (song), 20, 75, 141
Four Quartets: Alec Guinness radio broadcast, 23; circularity in, 4, 20; clearing rights for *Of Time and the City*, 141; Davies's films as homages to, 109–10; influence on Davies, 125–26; music and, 68–69; memory and nonlinearity in, 28–29; origins of, 5–6; stasis in, 18; structure of, 5–6; time and aging in, 109–10, 120–21
Free Cinema movement, 90–91, 96
Freudian definition of trauma, 29, 35
funding of Davies's films, 16

Garland, Judy, 71, 72
Gershwin, George, 66, 74
Gheorghiu, Angela, 25, 75
Gibbon, Lewis Grassic, 6
Gielgud, John, 45
Glasgow, 133
Gone with the Wind (1939), 106
Greater London Arts Association, 27
Great Expectations (1946), 103, 105, 139
Greenaway, Peter, 62
Grenfell, Joyce, 139
Grierson, John, 12, 24, 93
Guinness, Alec, 23, 104, 125

Hallelujah Now (novel), 12, 50, 59, 123n7
Happiest Days of Your Life, The (1950), 26, 103–4
Hart, Lorenz, 66, 75
Haynes, Todd, 10, 55, 100
He Who Hesitates (novel), 16
Hobbs, Christopher, 32, 77–78
Hoffmeister, Florian, 80, 146
homoeroticism in Davies's films, 36, 43–51, 94–95
Hope and Glory (1987), 13
Hopper, Edward, 80
House of Mirth, The (2000): as adaptation, 52–53; empty spaces in, 117–18; ending, 139–40; influence of painting on, 81–85; and John Singer Sargent, 81–83, 133; Lily Bart as queer figure, 43, 52–56; linearity of, 14; locations, 133; opening and closing images in, 106–8, 145; principal cast and crew of, 149–50; set design, 133–34; time in, 106–8, 116, 117–18
House of Mirth, The (novel), 53–54, 85
Houseman, A. E., 134
"How Long Has This Been Going On?" (song), 74
Hunt, Martita, 139

I Remember Mama (1948), 129
"It All Depends on You" (song), 65–66, 141–42

Jarman, Derek, 10, 89, 95
J. Arthur Rank Organization, 103–4
Jennings, Humphrey, 12, 23–24, 70, 91, 93
Jordan, Neil, 16
Julien, Issac, 10, 95

Kensington Street, 71, 78, 104, 145
Kern, Jerome, 66
Kiarostami, Abbas, 98
Kind Hearts and Coronets (1949), 26, 91
"kitchen-sink" dramas, 12, 90–94
Kubrick, Stanley, 7

Lady Agnew of Locknaw (painting), 82
Ladykillers, The (1955), 104
Lancashire, 78
Last, Bob, 124n8
Lee, Peggy, 20, 141
Leigh, Mike, 12, 62
Letter from an Unknown Woman (1948), 55, 129
Life of Oharu, The (1950), 53
lighting: in *The Deep Blue Sea*, 80; in *The Long Day Closes*, 78–79, 86–87; in *Madonna and Child*, 48; in *The Neon Bible*, 81
Listen to Britain (1942), 23–24, 70
Liszt, Franz, 75

Liverpool: architecture of, 18–22, 24; Davies's unwillingness to return, 144–45; history of, 22; in *Death and Transfiguration*, 64; in *The Long Day Closes*, 60, 77–78; in *Of Time and the City*, 15–16, 18–25, 75, 97; Toxteth riots, 22, 123n1; working class of, 24–25, 67–69
Loach, Ken, 62
Loneliness of the Long-Distance Runner, The (1962), 91
Long Day Closes, The (1992): aesthetic qualities of, 12–13, 77–79, 85–89; art direction, 77–79; autobiographical elements of, 26, 28–30, 39; camera perspective in, 104, 114–15; closing sequence, 122; color and lighting, 77–79; crucifixion shot, 36; death of father in, 42; empty spaces in, 114–15; and *Four Quartets*, 120–21; homosexual desire in, 42–45; influence of Dutch painting on, 78–79; Liverpool in, 22; movie references in, 60, 100, 102–5, 122; music in, 70–74; opening credits sequence, 120–21; opening scene, 103–6, 114–15; principal cast and crew of, 148–49; production of, 62; radical style of, 102–5; religion in, 35, 36; rug shot, 85–89, 134; sadomasochism in, 48; school bullying in, 31–33; time and, 108–9, 116, 120–23
Look Back in Anger (play), 93–94
Look Back in Anger (1958 film), 123n5
Los Angeles, 139–40
Love Is a Many-Splendored Thing (1955), 55, 100–101
Love Me or Leave Me (1955), 65, 142
"Love Song of J. Alfred Prufrock, The" (poem), 126

Mad About the Boy (unproduced Davies screenplay), 16
Madonna and Child (1980): death of father in, 42; homosexual desire in, 43; 48–51; morbidity of, 64; principal cast and crew of, 147; production, 27; sadomasochism in, 48–51
Magnificent Ambersons, The (1942), 105, 122

Mahler, Gustav, 75
Malick, Terrence, 7, 18
Mapplethorpe, Robert, 47
Marcello, Alessandro, 107
McBain, Ed, 16
Meet Me in St. Louis (1944), 71, 72, 105
melodrama, 55, 58, 100–101
Merchant-Ivory Productions, 12
Merifield, James, 146
Milkmaid, The (painting), 79
Miracle Worker, The (1962), 127
mise-en-scène in Davies's films, 76–85
Mizoguchi, Kenji, 53
"Molly Malone" (song), 70
Momma Don't Allow (1955), 91, 97
Montagu, Lord Edward, 45
Morning Walk (painting), 83
Mrs. Lloyd (painting), 85
Mullan, Peter, 146
"Music for the Royal Fireworks" (Handel), 25
music in Davies's films, 13, 63–76, 87–88; as counterpoint, 40, 64–66, 76, 101; classical music 75–76, 126; music clearances, 124n8, 140–42; musicals (Davies's films as), 67, 70–71, 97–98; popular music, 65–76
My Beautiful Laundrette (1985), 10
Myers, Ruth, 146
Myrbach, Felicien de, 18

National Film School, 27
National Film Theatre, 91
Neon Bible, The (1995): aesthetic qualities of, 14, 34–35, 80–81; as adaptation, 33–34; Aunt Mae as queer figure, 52; death of father in, 41–42; ending, 41–42; music in, 74–75; negative responses to, 34; principal cast and crew of, 149; radical style of, 105–6; religion in, 33–36; time in, 109, 116, 118–19; violence in, 41–42, 138
Neon Bible, The (novel), 33–36, 41, 52, 105, 118
Newman, Alfred, 103
New Queer Cinema, 95, 99–100, 115
1984 (1984), 130
nonlinearity in Davies's films, 29, 135–37

Norman, Jessye, 141
nostalgia: and aesthetics in Davies's films; 63–64; and conservatism in Davies's films, 89–90, 95–96, 100; and trauma, 29, 42
Nott-Bower, John, 45

Of Time and the City (2008): as unorthodox documentary, 15–16, 23–25; architecture in, 19–20; black and white, 30, 129; conservatism of, 89, 97; and digital video, 140; homosexual desire in, 45–47; and Humphrey Jennings, 23–24; Liverpool in, 18–25; movie love in, 100; music in, 24–25, 75; nonlinearity of, 116; narration in, 23; origins and production, 15–16, 20, 141; principal crew of, 150; queer space, 59; subjectivity of, 19–23
ontological properties of cinema, 113–14
Osborne, John, 93–94
O'Sullivan, Terry, 48, 142–43
Ozu, Yasujiro, 118, 128

painting and Davies's films, 78–85, 133
Papadopoulos, Solon, 20
photographic tableaux in Davies's films, 111–12
Poison (1991), 100
Porter, Cole, 66
Powell, Michael, 97–98
preproduction methods, 61–63
Presley, Elvis, 99
Prick Up Your Ears (1987), 10
Pumpkin Eater, The (1964), 127

queerness: of Davies's aesthetic, 60–61, 84–85, 98–106; of Davies's cinema, 6–11, 17, 60–61, 95–96, 98–106, 112–16; and melodrama, 57–58; of Lily Bart, 53–56, 84–85; and performance, 63; and artistic reappropriation, 98–100; temporality and time, 9, 88–89, 110–23; and trauma, 95–96, 99

radicalism of Davies's cinema, 89–90, 97–106
Radio 3, 141

Rattigan, Terence, 56, 58–59, 94–95, 135
realism in British cinema, 12, 90–94, 134–35
Red Shoes, The (1948), 103
Reisz, Karel, 91
Relph, Michael, 46
Rembrandt, 78
Repose (Nonchaloire) (painting), 83
Resnais, Alain, 18, 115
Reynolds, Debbie, 72–74
Reynolds, Joshua, 85
Richardson, Tony, 123n5
Robe, The (1953), 26, 100, 104, 129
Rodgers, Richard, 66, 75
"Roll Out the Barrel" (song), 24, 70
Room at the Top (1959), 91
Rossellini, Roberto, 115
Rowlands, Gena, 52, 74–75
Rutherford, Margaret, 103, 139

sadomasochistic homoeroticism in Davies's films, 46–51
Saturday Night and Sunday Morning (1960), 91
screenwriting, 61–62
Sebastiane (1976), 95
Separate Tables (1958), 94
Shadow of a Doubt (1943), 129
Shock of the New, The (1980), 128
"Shropshire Lad, A" (Butterworth), 88, 134
Sim, Alastair, 139
sing-alongs, 13, 58–59, 67–71, 75
Singer Sargent, John, 81–85, 133
Singin' in the Rain (1952), 26, 60, 123n4, 128
Sisters of the Gion (1936), 53
Snow, Michael, 98
South Bank Show, The (1992), 65
Stafford, Jo, 69–70
"Stardust" (song), 71–72, 104
St. George's Hall, 18, 24, 140
Still Life (play), 57
Street of Shame (1956), 53
Sullivan, Arthur, 122
Sullivan, Frances L., 139
Summer (painting), 84–85
Sunset Boulevard (1950), 110

Index | 163

Sunset Song (novel), 16, 128, 146
Swoon (1992), 100

"Taking a Chance on Love" (song), 40, 138
"Tammy" (song), 72–74
Tarkovsky, Andrei, 7
Tarr, Béla, 98
Taste of Honey, A (1961), 91
Taverner, John, 75
Technicolor, 77, 91, 131
Terence Davies Trilogy, The (1976–83): black and white in, 76, 129–30; homoeroticism in, 47–51, 95; morbidity of, 64; music in, 64–66; nonlinearity in, 27, 29, 116; origins of, 12; production of each film, 27; realism of, 90; religion in, 33; time in, 108–9. See also *Children*; *Madonna and Child*; *Death and Transfiguration*
Thatcher, Margaret, 89
This Sporting Life (1963), 91
Tom of Finland, 47
Toole, John Kennedy, 14, 33–35, 41, 52, 105, 118
Toxteth riots, 22, 123n1

Tsai Ming-liang, 98
Twentieth Century-Fox fanfare, 103–4, 106

Vermeer, Johannes, 78–79, 133
Victim (1961), 45–46
violence on screen 39–41, 127, 137–38

Walker Art Gallery (Liverpool), 133
Walk to the Paradise Garden, The (radio play), 123n7
Warhol, Andy, 10, 100
"Watch and Pray" (Branesti), 25
Watteau, Antoine, 84–85
Waves, The (radio play), 123n7
We Are the Lambeth Boys (1958), 91
Weisz, Rachel, 52, 80
Wharton, Edith, 14, 52–55, 81, 139
While I Live (1947), 128
Wizard of Oz, The (1939), 36
Wolfenden Report, 45
Wong Kar-wai, 7, 18
World War II, 20, 24, 114

"You Belong to Me" (song), 69–70
Young at Heart (1954), 137, 142

Michael Koresky is the staff writer of The Criterion Collection, cofounder and co-editor-in-chief of the online film magazine *Reverse Shot,* and was contributing writer to the books *Olivier Assayas* and *Essential Art House: 50 Years of Janus Films.*

Books in the series Contemporary Film Directors

Nelson Pereira dos Santos
Darlene J. Sadlier

Abbas Kiarostami
Mehrnaz Saeed-Vafa and Jonathan Rosenbaum

Joel and Ethan Coen
R. Barton Palmer

Claire Denis
Judith Mayne

Wong Kar-wai
Peter Brunette

Edward Yang
John Anderson

Pedro Almodóvar
Marvin D'Lugo

Chris Marker
Nora Alter

Abel Ferrara
Nicole Brenez, translated by Adrian Martin

Jane Campion
Kathleen McHugh

Jim Jarmusch
Juan Suárez

Roman Polanski
James Morrison

Manoel de Oliveira
John Randal Johnson

Neil Jordan
Maria Pramaggiore

Paul Schrader
George Kouvaros

Jean-Pierre Jeunet
Elizabeth Ezra

Terrence Malick
Lloyd Michaels

Sally Potter
Catherine Fowler

Atom Egoyan
Emma Wilson

Albert Maysles
Joe McElhaney

Jerry Lewis
Chris Fujiwara

Jean-Pierre and Luc Dardenne
Joseph Mai

Michael Haneke
Peter Brunette

Alejandro González Iñárritu
Celestino Deleyto and Maria del Mar Azcona

Lars von Trier
Linda Badley

Hal Hartley
Mark L. Berrettini

François Ozon
Thibaut Schilt

Steven Soderbergh
Aaron Baker

Mike Leigh
Sean O'Sullivan

D.A. Pennebaker
Keith Beattie

Jacques Rivette
Mary M. Wiles

Kim Ki-duk
Hye Seung Chung

Philip Kaufman
  Annette Insdorf

Richard Linklater
  David T. Johnson

David Lynch
  Justus Nieland

John Sayles
  David R. Shumway

Dario Argento
  L. Andrew Cooper

Todd Haynes
  Rob White

Christian Petzold
  Jaimey Fisher

Spike Lee
  Todd McGowan

Terence Davies
  Michael Koresky

The University of Illinois Press
is a founding member of the
Association of American University Presses.

_____

Composed in 10/13 New Caledonia
with Helvetica Neue display
by Lisa Connery
at the University of Illinois Press
Manufactured by Cushing-Malloy, Inc.

University of Illinois Press
1325 South Oak Street
Champaign, IL 61820-6903
www.press.uillinois.edu